The School Psychologist's Handbook

by

Arthur A. Attwell, Ed.D.

WESTERN PSYCHOLOGICAL SERVICES
PUBLISHERS AND DISTRIBUTORS
12031 WILSHIRE BOULEVARD
LOS ANGELES, CALIFORNIA 90025
A DIVISION OF MANSON WESTERN CORPORATION

The School Psychologists' Handbook

Library of Congress Catalog Number: 76-182925

International Standard Book Number: 0-87424-122-7

Table of Contents

About the Author

Dr. Arthur Attwell is Professor of Educational Psychology and chairman of the Department at California State University, Los Angeles. In addition, he is a consultant in research, guidance and special education for various public and private agencies. A veteran school psychologist, he is the author of "The Retarded Child: Answers to Questions Parents Ask," in addition to more than 50 other monographs and articles relating to school psychology and exceptional children.

Foreword

In the short history of school psychology there has continued to exist a formidable gap between theory and practice. This gap has been considerably narrowed with the publication of this handbook.

Anyone acquainted with or beginning in a professional career in school psychology will profit immeasurably from the skilled and realistic approach taken by Dr. Attwell in defining the responsibilities, tools and practices that are important in allowing this science to make a contribution to the educative process.

This book fulfills a dual need both as a text for those students preparing themselves for this profession, and as a resource book for those already actively engaged. Outstanding uniqueness evolves from pointing new directions in the field of school psychology as well as the distillation of those practices which have proven most successful out of the wisdom of the past. *The School Psychologist's Handbook* unerringly focuses on the essentials in a world that intimidates the mind with the profuseness of irrelevant facts and information.

GUY CHAPMAN, ED. D.
Director of Special Services
Tulare County Superintendent
of Schools Office
California

Introduction

There are many things this handbook is *not*. It does not pretend to be, for example, a thorough treatise on prescriptive teaching, such as those by Peter, Bruekner and Bond, Otto & McMenemy, etc. It is most certainly *not* an important *text* on school psychology as is Magary, or on clinical management, as Bakwin or Verville.

It *is*, however, intended to be a handy, practical guide for the new or experienced school psychologist, who might wish to turn to a specific topic for a "starting place" in the identification or treatment of a school difficulty. It should also be useful for the school psychologist to locate current information regarding placement criteria and procedures for special education classes. It has been written from a school orientation, so that it will provide the psychologist with meaningful, practical recommendations he might make to the teacher.

Because the writer is more experienced with California education, especially with regard to special education, this state has been frequently cited. Placement procedures would vary, of course, from state to state, so the reader should consult his local state education code for the specific procedures in his state.

Appreciation is expressed to Dr. Robert Benoit of California State College, Los Angeles, Dr. Robert Valett of Fresno State College for the use of their material in Chapter I and to Dr. Shirlee Davis of California State College, Los Angeles and Mrs. June Teske of the Los Angeles County Superintendent of Schools Office for editing the material used in the Handbook.

ARTHUR A. ATTWELL
Los Angeles, Calif., Feb., 1972

1. The Emerging Role of the School Psychologist

Defining the Role

An important factor in the success of any school psychologist is the degree to which his role has been defined, for it is this role definition which furnishes the parameters within which he can establish priorities and distribute his time. Generally, there are several major sources for role definition and job description. The four primary sources are the legal definition, the professional description, the local district definition, and the psychologist's own personal job definition, into which he incorporates his own philosophy.*

Legal Definition

The legal definition of the function of the school psychologist is found in each state's Education Code. This code usually states that the school psychologist is the only person who has the authority to administer an individual examination for the purpose of placing a child in special classes, and is the only person who can legally classify children and recommend them for special classes.

Professional Definition

Professional groups traditionally seek refined definitions of their disciplines. In the case of the school psychologist, the groups outstanding in this respect are the American Psychological Association, the newly-formed National Association of School Psychologists, and the various State Associations of School Psychologists. These organizations have expended considerable effort in defining the role of the school psychologist, and have developed thoughtful and comprehensive role descriptions (Magary, *School Psychological Services,* Prentice-Hall, 1967, pp 2-3).

This handbook does not discuss the role of the school psychologist in detail, but merely points out to the psychologist the importance of role definition and the various sources to which the psychologist can turn for guidance in this respect. The reader is referred to Magary's comprehensive book for a more exhaustive treatment of this subject.

---

*Acknowledgment is given to Dr. Robert Benoit, Chairman, Dept. of Pupil Personnel Services, Calif. State College, Los Angeles.

District Definition

While the State Codes define the legal aspect, and the professional associations the ideal, it is the local district which gives the actual operational definition and determines to the greatest extent just how the psychologist will spend most of his time.

The psychologist's employing district is required to define his role at least partially in terms of the State Code's legal requirements, but beyond that the district definitions vary greatly. The wise psychologist becomes well acquainted with the way in which the district defines his role. Many times, a lack of mutual understanding in the beginning leads to conflicting and unrealistic demands being made on the psychologist. To prevent this kind of situation, the psychologist should clearly understand what his employing district expects, and what he expects from the district. The all too common practice, for example, of expecting *numbers* of case studies can quickly lead to the problem of quantity versus quality. The writer has long resisted attempts to specify any given optimal number of case studies per day or week. Certain forms of testing can be done with relative speed, whereas others, such as initial screening and many school behavior referrals, take vastly longer.

Personal Definition

In the final analysis, it is the psychologist's own philosophy which guides his everyday behavior as a professional. It is incumbent upon every professional school psychologist to examine his personal attitudes, beliefs, values, and goals. In view of the terrific external pressures and valences which exist, only the professional person who knows himself will be able to integrate these external definitions of his role with a personal philosophy to develop a viable personal conception to guide his own functioning.

The psychologist whose role definition is chiefly from external sources is easy prey to the frequently conflicting demands of others. He may be in constant conflict over what to do first, and may be constantly tempted to function in ways which violate his own conscience. This is not to say that the psychologist functions independently of those around him, but rather in an integrated way, which takes into consideration the needs of others, while integrating them into an overall unique pattern of functioning.

Implementing the Job

Setting Priorities. There will always be more things for the psychologist to do than he *can* do. It is imperative that he have a system of priorities by which he can decide what is to be done first. Once it becomes known that he "oils the hinges which squeak the loudest," his effectiveness is minimized. This system of priorities will obviously be based largely on his integrated job description.

Time Budgeting. The psychologist must learn to budget his time. Always appearing to be in a hurry is annoying to others if they need the psychologist's full and undivided attention (which may be, in the final analysis, a primary service of the psychologist). A frequent teacher complaint about psychologists is that they "never seem to have enough time," or that they "give a test, but never follow-up." It behooves the psychologist to pay attention to the needs of his constituents, and not appear to always be rushing off to something more important. Only effective time budgeting makes this possible.

Developing Referral Procedures. The manner in which a case is referred to the school psychologist may have much to do with how effectively he is able to deal with the situation. Many teachers resent filling out a long referral form which they feel is often irrelevant and unread. An objective, consistent referral procedure is an important part of any case, and should be given careful thought.

Scheduling conference time with the teacher, and allowing ample opportunity for him to tell the psychologist what is known about the pupil, may preclude the need for actual testing. It may also provide an opportunity to explore some of the teacher's attitudes about the pupil. At any rate, an important first step following receipt of the referral is a conference with the teacher and a careful observation of the pupil in his classroom setting.

The School Psychologist as a Psychoeducational Consultant*

With the increased development of new programs, a need has developed for school psychologists versed in diagnosis, remediation, and psycho-educational programming. Although these "psycho-educational consultants" may be obtained by retraining teachers, counselors, or curriculum personnel, the most probable source is from the field of school psychology. Specific functions of the psycho-educational specialist include:

1. Aid teachers and administrators in understanding the behavioral characteristics of pupils with learning disorders; help them to screen, identify, and refer such pupils. Participate in and conduct district and local school workshops and in-service training classes.

2. Consult with and train special diagnostic teachers in the use of individual psycho-educational evaluation instruments such as the Developmental Survey, Psycho-educational Inventory, Frostig, Spache, WRAT, etc.

3. Aid teachers in parent conferences, pupil evaluation sessions, and subsequent pupil profiling of learning strengths and weaknesses.

4. Consult with teachers on the development and use of weekly lesson plans and daily pupil learning prescriptions. Consult with teachers on other related matters as requested by them.

5. Lead school case conferences on individual children at the beginning of the year, for the purpose of program planning.

6. Serve as a weekly consultant to an assigned group counseling meeting of special teachers.

7. Conduct special follow-up evaluations of pupils as needed, using such instruments as the Lincoln-Oseretsky Scale, Ayers, ITPA, Kephart, and standard psychological instruments. Write specific remedial psycho-educational prescriptions, confer with teachers, demonstrate recommendations, and provide follow-up consultations.

8. Aid the teacher in group consultation with parents concerning the nature of learning disabilities and the general and specific remedial program involved.

9. Consult with the teacher in the development of a behavior modification system based on principles of learning and an applied social reinforcement system.

10. Consult with parents in the development of understanding of the pupil's learning problem, the nature of their child's prescription, the behavior modification system employed, and their own involvement as parents.

*Extracted with the speaker's permission from "The Evaluation and Programming of Learning Disabilities," presented by Dr. Robert Valett at the conference on the assessment of multi-handicapped children, Los Angeles, 1968.

11. Consult with individual pupils regarding the nature of their learning and behavior problems and counsel them as necessary.

12. Conduct applied research in the school and classroom.

13. Consult with principals, directors, and administrators regarding the organization, development, and improvement of preventive, remedial, and special education programs in assigned schools.

14. Serve as liaison and consultant to other professionals involved, such as speech therapists, audiometrists, nurses, physicians, and appropriate agencies.

2. Referrals and Report Writing

Intra-District Referrals

Most school districts have standard forms to be used by the teacher or administrator for referring a pupil for a psychological study. These referral forms are usually initiated by the teacher and countersigned by the principal. The form need not be elaborate; in fact, many teachers object to long forms which require much information not always relevant to the particular referral.

Perhaps the most practical form is one which contains only the basic information regarding the pupil, such as his name, birthdate, grade level, previous test results, and an informal statement of the pupil's problem to be considered. The following simple form has been used by the writer for several years.

Some districts prefer the use of a more informative pupil referral form, with the philosophy that the teacher referring the pupil usually has the needed information at hand, thus saving the psychologist much time in locating and recording the information. An example of one of these forms is shown on pages 4 & 5.

Request for Psychological Evaluation

Name of Child_____ Birthdate_____

School_____ Grade_____ Date_____

Teacher_____How long has child been
in your school?

Previous Test Results: Group _____Date_____

_____Date_____

Individual _____Date_____

_____Date

Reason for the Referral _____

_____

_____

_____

Referred by_____ Approved by_____ Date_____
(Administrator)

Inter-District Referrals

When psychological services or special education programs are provided on an inter-district agreement or by the local county superintendent of schools office, the referral forms must now become more formal. The forms at the end of this chapter have been successfully used by the Los Angeles County Superintendent of Schools Office and are included through the courtesy of this office.

Report Writing

The psychological report is intended to communicate to the reader the findings and recommendations of the study and should contain any relevant information relating to the total picture of the pupil involved. The report is usually intended for use by the pupil's teacher and/or administrator, so should contain specific recommendations for the classroom management of the problem. There is an important trend toward including classroom prescriptive techniques, and any report written for the teacher's use should contain this information.

STUDENT REFERRAL FOR PSYCHOLOGICAL SERVICES

By
William A. McClain

Published by

WESTERN PSYCHOLOGICAL SERVICES
PUBLISHERS AND DISTRIBUTORS
12031 WILSHIRE BOULEVARD
LOS ANGELES, CALIFORNIA 90025

A DIVISION OF MANSON WESTERN CORPORATION

Referred by:_____ Position:_____ Date:_____

Instructions: Try to provide **all** the information requested. **Circle** the correct information when alternative answers, printed in bold type, have been provided. **Write in** the correct information wherever lines have been provided for this purpose. You may not have all the information requested, in which case leave the answer blank.

I. PERSONAL DATA

Child's name:_____ Age:_____ Date of birth:_____
Home address:_____ Telephone No.:_____
School:_____ Teacher's name:_____ Grade:_____ Room No.:_____

II. REASON FOR REFERRAL

Give brief descriptive statement of problem (e.g. underachievement, aggressiveness, etc.):_____

Briefly state what you consider to be the reason for child's problem:_____
_____
_____

III. PRECIPITATING BEHAVIOR

Briefly, but specifically, describe the behavior, actions, and circumstances that resulted in this **referral** being made:_____
_____
_____

If this behavior was not observed by you, state who observed it:_____

IV. PERTINENT HISTORY AND BACKGROUND INFORMATION

Family

1. Child lives with: **Both parents   Mother   Father   Guardian   Other:**_____
2. Others living in the home: **Grandmother   Grandfather   Stepmother   Stepfather   Others:**_____
3. Parents are: **Living together   Separated   Divorced   Deceased   Only mother is alive   Only father is alive**
4. Father is alive: **Yes   No**   If no, when did father die:_____ Cause of death:_____
5. Mother is alive: **Yes   No**   If no, when did mother die:_____ Cause of death:_____
6. Language(s) spoken at home: **English   Spanish   Other:**_____
7. Parental attitude toward child is (e.g. rejecting, accepting, etc.):_____
8. Child has had following traumatic experiences and/or stresses (e.g. deaths, accidents, illnesses of child or others in family, etc.):_____
9. Child was adopted: **Yes   No**   If yes, at what age:_____
10. Mother is employed: **Yes   No**   If yes, where:_____ Hours:_____
11. Father is employed: **Yes   No**   If yes, where:_____ Hours:_____
12. Who is responsible for child's discipline: **Father and mother   Father   Mother   Guardian   Neighbor   Other:**_____
13. Briefly describe the type of discipline used:_____
14. List the other children in the child's family who are now alive:

Name	Sex	Age	Grade	Health

1 2 3 4 5 6 7 8 9

15. List the other children in the child's family who have died:

Name	Sex	Age at death	Date of death	Cause of death

16. Other information about the child or family which might be important or significant:_____

Medical

1. The child has been hospitalized: **Yes No**   If yes, when:_____Reason:_____
2. The child has had surgery: **Yes No** If yes, when:_____Reason:_____
3. The child currently has physical problems: **Yes No** If yes, what:_____
4. The child wears eyeglasses: **Yes No**
5. The child uses a hearing aid: **Yes No**
6. The child is currently taking the special medication: **Yes No** If yes, describe the medication:_____

Academic

1. Child's exact age when starting first grade:_____Years_____Months
2. Pupil has failed or repeated a grade: **Yes No** If yes, describe:_____
3. Child has generally gotten along well in school: **Yes No**
4. Child's approximate grade point average to date:_____
5. The child has done poorly in the following areas:_____
   _____How long:_____
6. The child's mental ability is:_____
      Intelligence test results are: Group_____Individual_____
7. The child's achievement is:_____
      Achievement test results are:_____
8. The child's vocational aptitude is:_____
      Vocational aptitude test results are:_____
9. The child's personality is:_____
      Personality test results are:_____
10. The child has been to a psychiatrist or clinical psychologist: **Yes   No**   If yes, give results of this
      experience:_____
11. The child has excessive absences or tardiness in school history: **Yes No** If yes, when:_____
12. The child's instructional reading level is:_____

V. ATTITUDE AND RELATIONSHIP TOWARD ADULTS AND PEERS

Child's attitude toward teachers is:_____
Child's attitude toward parents is:_____
Child's attitude toward other adults is:_____
Child's attitude toward peers in school:_____
Child's attitude toward peers outside of school:_____

VI. CLASSROOM MEASURES TAKEN TO RESOLVE THIS PROBLEM

_____
_____
_____
_____
_____

VII. YOUR IMPRESSION OF THE CHILD AS A PERSON

_____
_____
_____
_____
_____

VIII. REFERRAL OBJECTIVES

Please answer the following questions:_____
Please provide the following assistance:_____
Comments:_____

The following report form is currently being used by the Los Angeles County Superintendent of Schools Office.

Report of Psychological Testing

Name of Child:_____ Date:____

Date of Birth:_____

Date of Test:_____ Test Used:_____

School:_____ Results:_____

Examiner:_____ Test Used:_____

Range of Successes_____ Results:_____

Previous Test Results

Date	Test	Results

Comments in the areas of background information, current information, behavior during testing, results of testing, areas of strength and weaknesses, summary, conclusions, recommendations:

_____

_____

_____

_____

Some Do's and Don'ts in Report Writing

1. Keep the report readable and understandable so that the reader can tell exactly what recommendations the writer has outlined for the pupil. Do not strive for literary style. The primary purpose of the report is to communicate.
2. Unless the case is very complex, keep the report as short as possible. A report of one or two pages is usually sufficient to include the pertinent data needed. Avoid repetition, trivial gossip, suppositions, or assumptions not documented.
3. Avoid the use of terms which are vague or which can have more than one meaning to the reader, such as "poorly adjusted," "well-behaved," etc.
4. If the writer feels that the test score is invalid, he should state this in the report. There are often many factors — physiological, environmental, emotional — which can invalidate a test, and it is certainly not to the discredit of the writer for him to consider a test score invalid.

5. Avoid the use of the first person. Rather, refer to yourself as "the writer," "the examiner," etc.
6. The report should be directed toward the problem stated in the referral. However, because the school psychological report usually becomes a part of the pupil's permanent record and may be read in the future by people from various agencies or disciplines, it should contain related information which might be of assistance to doctors, reading or speech clinics, special class teachers, etc.
7. Before writing the report, the findings should be discussed with the teacher. The teacher should never be "surprised" by the findings and recommendations of the psychological report, but should be involved in the planning.
8. If the teacher and psychologist disagree on the recommendations, this can be stated in the report, listing the opinions of each. This is an essential aspect of professional rapport; further, it is the only honest way to be objective in terms of helping the pupil.

Report of Psychological Testing

Name of Child: *Weaver, Mary*   Date: 5-10-70
Date of Birth: 2-6-62
Date of Test: 4-11-70   Test Used: Binet, L-M
School: Lincoln (TMR) Results: CA8-2; MA 4-9; IQ 56
Examiner: J. Jones Test Used: Goodenough Drawing
Range of Successes: III through V yr. Results: MA 4-6

Previous Test Results

Date	Test	Results
11-3-67	Binet, L-M	CA 5-9; MA 3-0; IQ 47

_____

_____

_____

_____

_____

_____

_____

_____

Reason for Referral: To obtain current psychological information relative to Mary's optimal placement. Mary has been in the current TMR program 2½ years, and has been making steady progress. Mary's teacher suspects that the girl may be eligible for placement in an EMR class.

REPORT OF PSYCHOLOGICAL EVALUATION

(To be completed by school psychologist. Use additional pages as needed.)

Date _____

Name _____ Birth Date _____ District _____

Group and individual intelligence test results in chronological order, beginning with earliest testing:

Date	Test	Results
_____	_____	_____
_____	_____	_____
_____	_____	_____
_____	_____	_____
_____	_____	_____

Description of present intellectual functioning:

Description of present motor skills:

Description of present language and communication skills:

Description of social/emotional adjustment:

Specific Learning or Behavior Disorders	Typical Behavior Indicating Disorders	Relationship of Disorder to Expected School Achievement
_____	_____	_____
_____	_____	_____
_____	_____	_____
_____	_____	_____
_____	_____	_____

Is the pupil's behavior inimical to the welfare of other pupils? _____

Specific Recommendations Regarding Methods and Services to be Provided	Anticipated Results
_____	_____
_____	_____
_____	_____
_____	_____
_____	_____
_____	_____

By _____ Title _____ Date _____

LOS ANGELES COUNTY SUPERINTENDENT OF SCHOOLS
DIVISION OF SPECIAL EDUCATION

REPORT OF EDUCATIONAL CASE STUDY
(To be completed by teacher)

Name of Pupil _____ Program _____ Date _____

Birth Date _____ Age _____ School _____

Date of entry into class _____ Teacher _____

Achievement Test Scores:

Date	Test	Results	Date	Test	Results

Areas of educational strength:

Areas of Educational Handicap	Steps Taken to Assist Pupil	Results of Assistance

Describe the ability of the pupil to function in present classroom (include description of program expectancies and academic standards):

Describe present emotional and social functioning (include pupil's reaction to success and failure):

(For additional comments use reverse side)
Recommendations:

8

SEC 5 1/70

REPORT OF ADMISSION COMMITTEE
(For County Office Use Only)

___ New Referral
___ Reevaluation
___ Workshop

pil _____ District _____ Date _____
    Last (legal)   First

rthdate _____ Age _____ Program _____ Sex _____

hool _____

Action of the Committee

e Admission Committee has considered the case of the above-named pupil and has acted as noted below:

___ 1. The following additional information is needed before a recommendation can be made:

_____

    Reason: _____

    Probable date of restaffing: _____

___ 2. Trial placement recommended (MR only): _____

    Reason: _____

_____

    Probable date or restaffing: _____

___ 3. Placement recommended. On waiting list_____ Date enrolled _____

___ 4. Continued placement recommended Yes ☐ No ☐ (Yes or No) Last day of attendance_____

___ 5. Workshop entry date _____

___ 6. Return to district of residence with recommendation for the following program:

    Regular class: ____ EMR: ____ TMR: ____ EH: ____ PH: ____ DCHM: ____ Other: _____

    Reason: _____

    Last day of Attendance _____

___ 7. Other professional recommendations: _____

    Reason: _____

_____

mments:

hool Administrator _____ Teacher _____

hool Psychologist _____ Other _____
                                       Signature and Title

ysician _____ Other _____
                                       Signature and Title

hool Nurse _____ Other _____
                                       Signature and Title

port of dissent from majority opinion attached _____
                                     Yes or No

tribution:
ounty Office (white copy)
istrict of residence (yellow copy)
rogram school (green copy)
ther (pink copy)

: 18.3.7/71

Los Angeles County Superintendent of Schools Office
Division of Special Education

PHYSICIAN'S RECOMMENDATION FOR PHYSICAL EDUCATION AND OTHER PHYSICAL ACTIVITIES

Date _____

Dear Physician:

All pupils enrolled in the public schools participate in physical education activities which are designed to meet their growth and developmental needs. In addition, many pupils participate in other types of activity, such as intramural programs, interschool athletics, band, and drill teams. To identify specific needs of each pupil, the physician, parents, and school personnel must work cooperatively. Will you please provide us with the information listed below so that we can provide appropriate activities for: _____

(Pupil's Name)

Findings and Recommendations to the School

I have examined _____ and find the following handicap

(Pupil's Name)

(if any): _____

_____

_____

_____

_____

_____

_____

_____

_____

The condition has been diagnosed as: _____

_____

_____

_____

I recommend the following:

_____ 1. No restriction on any type of activity

_____ 2. Participation in all activities (intramural and other activities in addition to physical education), with the exception of inter-school athletics

_____ 3. No restriction on activities in physical education

4. Adaptations in physical education to fit individual needs:

_____ a. Little running or jumping

_____ b. No running or jumping

_____ c. No activities involving body contact

_____ d. Exercises designed for rehabilitation

_____ e. Strenuous conditioning exercises

5. Other adaptations: (Specify) _____

_____

I recommend the adaptation for: _____ two weeks, _____ one month, _____ three months, _____ six month

Date _____   Signature _____

Name _____   Address _____

(please print)

Please mail this form to: Admission Consultant, Division of Special Education
Los Angeles County Superintendent of Schools Office
1851 South Westmoreland Avenue
Los Angeles, California 90006

This form conforms to requirements in Education Code Section 11906.

SEC 138/71   10

Admission Consultant, Division of Special Education
Los Angeles County Superintendent of Schools Office
1851 South Westmoreland Avenue, Los Angeles, California 90006

Date _____

is to inform you of the following referral:

Last Name (legal)	First	Middle	Sex	Program Recommended

Present School	Teacher's Name	Class Assignment

Birth Date	Birth Place	Verification of Birth Date

Father's Name	Occupation/Place of Employment	Business Phone	Home Phone

Mother's Name	Occupation/Place of Employment	Business Phone	Home Phone

whom does
l live? _____

Name	Relationship	Address	Phone

ired Immunizations
fied   NO ☐   YES ☐

		Agency	Phone
Date	By	Social Worker	
		Address	

Language in Home	Persons Living in Home

of other children in home _____

gious exemption   YES ☐   NO ☐   Court restraining order   YES ☐   NO ☐

icapping Conditions _____

SCHOOL HISTORY

ge	Grade	School	District	City and State

osures

_____ Report of District Admission Committee

_____ Report of Educational Case Study

_____ Medical Report/Certification

_____ Health and Developmental History

_____ Report of Psychological Evaluation

_____ Otologic Examination

_____ Parent consent for county placement
and commitment for transportation (EH only)

_____
Person Making Referral

_____
Title

_____
School District

he event that this pupil is accepted into the county program, authorization is granted for him to attend the
ommended special education class.

Date	Signature of Parent or Guardian

Date	Signature of Superintendent or Authorized Representative

s permit will remain in force until revoked by the district, or the child is declared ineligible by a County
ce Admission Committee.

(To be completed by County Office)

ort of preliminary interview with parents: By _____

TRIBUTION:

hite Copy   -- County Office
ellow Copy   -- Psychologist
reen Copy   -- Administrator
ink Copy   -- Physician
lue Copy   -- Other

Date _____

11

11.2-11.4/71

Current Information: Mary is an attractive, outgoing, verbal, normal-appearing girl of 8-2 with poor gross motor coordination. She has an awkward gait, and frequently falls when running. She has a diagnosis of "organicity associated with birth injuries" (Dr. Cutler, San Gabriel).

Mary's speech is relatively clear and distinct, and she uses complex sentences properly. She can identify colors, print her first and last names legibly, and can count to ten, relating numbers to objects. Mary contributes to class discussion, and is considered popular with her peers.

The parents are described as interested, intelligent, and cooperative. Mary is their only child.

Behavior During Examination: Mary was cooperative and helpful during the examination, frequently putting away test items for the examiner. She was able to sit for relatively long periods of time and volunteered much relevant conversation. Her behavior was somewhat infantile and gleeful at times, however, considering her mature speech and mannerisms.

Areas of Strengths and Weaknesses: Mary obtained her highest scores in the areas of verbal comprehension and vocabulary, passing the Vocabulary subtest at the VI year level, 1½ years above her mental age. Her weakest areas were the performance items. She was unable to complete the picture of a man, copy a square, or assemble the Patience Rectangles at the V year level.

Summary: Mary's current IQ score of 56 is significantly higher than her previous score of 47, and suggests that she is more than maintaining her rate of intellectual development. She is continuing to develop socially, as well. Though she has made little progress in the areas of gross motor functioning (running, skipping, etc.), her printing is legible, and she is now able to handle a primary pencil with relative ease.

Recommendations: The writer recommends that Mary be considered for placement in a class for the Educable Mentally Retarded next September. Meanwhile, continued emphasis on pre-academic skills should prove helpful in preparing her for this move. Mary's greatest need is in the area of neuro-muscular skills. Tasks such as cutting, pasting, tracing, printing, etc., should be encouraged as much as is feasible. Other visual-motor exercises, such as the use of the rail-board, mazes, the Frostig materials, etc., should also aid in remediating Mary's coordination difficulties.

Report of Psychological Testing

Name of Child: *Jordan, Charles*   Date: 5-10-70
Date of Birth: 11-14-62
Date of Test: 4-15-70   Test Used: W.I.S.C.
School: Vandalia (2nd grade)
Results: VQ 113; PQ 117; FSIQ 116
Examiner: J. Jones   Test Used: W.R.A.T.
Range of Successes: - - - -
Results: Rdng. 3.3; Spll. 2.9; Ar. 2.8

Previous Test Results

Date	Test	Results
None available		

Reason for Referral: Mr. and Mrs. Jordan feel that Charles is "bored" with school, that the school work is too easy for him, and have requested that their boy be accelerated to the 3rd grade at this time, so that he can go to the 4th grade in September.

Current Information: Charles is an alert, confident, slightly-built, verbal boy of 7-5, who moved to Vandalia last month with his family. The parents are intelligent and affluent. They are described by the teacher as interested and cooperative, but somewhat over-anxious about the boy's progress and future.

Charles is currently reading at the 3rd grade level. He knows his multiplication tables through 5, and is able to borrow and to carry with relative ease. He uses manuscript printing only, except for his name, which he can write legibly. His teacher describes him as an "avid reader" and a good worker in class.

Behavior During the Examination: Rapport was considered as excellent, and Charles obviously enjoyed the attention. He volunteered much relevant conversation, and answered even simple information questions in great detail.

Areas of Strengths and Weaknesses: This boy has a rather even profile of abilities, with all areas at or above the average range. His WISC profile of scaled scores is as follows:

Verbal (VQ 113)		*Performance* (PQ 117)	
Information	12	Picture Completion	10
Comprehension	12	Picture Arrangement	11
Arithmetic	11	Block Design	14
Similarities	13	Object Assembly	13
Vocabulary	14	Coding	14
Digit Span	10		

Summary and Recommendations: Charles is a 2nd grade boy with Bright-Normal intelligence who is achieving academically and socially in the top group in his class.

Though Charles could most probably eventually succeed academically if he were accelerated to the 3rd grade at this time, the writer feels there are several factors which militate against acceleration.

1. Charles is a slightly-built youngster, small for his CA of 7-5; further, he is one of the youngest children in his class.

2. The teacher does not see the classroom boredom described by the parents. The boy appears happy in class, works to capacity, and is given work commensurate with his ability.

3. There are 3 or 4 pupils in class who have academic and intellectual ability comparable to Charles', and who are older and larger than Charles. This would be even more evident in the 3rd grade, if he were to be accelerated.

4. Charles does not use cursive writing, and is not considered by his teacher to be ready for 4th grade arithmetic in September.

It is recommended that the teacher and the writer have a conference with Mr. and Mrs. Jordan, and to explain that because of the factors listed above, an acceleration of their boy at this time would not appear to be in his best interests.

3. Remediation of Learning Difficulties in Subject Matter

The school psychologist's emerging role as psycho-educational consultant requires that he be able not only to identify the nature of the pupil's learning difficulty, but that he be able to offer concrete suggestions to the teacher regarding the remediation of the problem. The broad process of remediation involves several preliminary but inter-related steps. Diagnosis and remediation are actually parts of the same process, for an investigation of one is the initiation of the other. The diagnosis and remediation of learning disorders involves the following logical steps, each of which is a part of the total picture of remediation.

1. The teacher identifies learning deficiencies in the child, and refers the child to the school psychologist when these deficiencies are markedly below the child's estimated abilities.

2. The psychologist determines the child's level of functioning and decides whether the child is functioning *below* his level or merely *at* his level. If the child *is* achieving below his intellectual level, an investigation is made as to whether the disability is general or specific.

3. The *causes* are now considered. The problems may include physiological (visual, hearing, neurological or perceptual disorders, prolonged illnesses, etc.), emotional (school or home tensions, phobias, etc.), social (poor peer relations, inadequate social adjustments, etc.), intellectual (retarded rate of maturation, mental retardation, etc.), educational (faulty learning habits, negative attitudes toward school or the teacher, inter-district transfers, etc.), or motivational (self-concept, poor learning set, etc.).

4. A diagnosis of the preliminary factors involved in the learning difficulty follows. Which one or more of the above presents the major cause of the problem? Is the factor one which *can* be remediated? (Mental retardation, for example, can not). The treatment is valid only when the diagnosis has been adequate.

5. The educative process is adapted, insofar as possible, to the individual needs of the pupil. The easiest solution is found when the learner has difficulties simply in a specific area, and the remediation can be directed toward the weak (or missing) skill.

6. The evaluation must be ongoing. The pupil should be aware of the plan, and must see his progress, however small.

Most teachers have at their disposal the various texts and teacher manuals which offer help for the child with difficulties. There are innumerable texts which offer specific remediation at a more detailed level, such as Brueckner & Bond and others. This chapter offers suggestions of a starting place from which the teacher might direct his attention.*

---

*Acknowledgement is given to the graduate students in the writer's School Psychology class at California State College, Los Angeles who offered many of the suggestions listed in this and the following chapter.

READING

Reading: Diagnosis of General Abilities

As with any academic area, the diagnosis of reading problems must not only determine the general problem, but must also indicate the specific areas of the reading difficulty. A proper diagnosis also suggests where and how the improvement can be brought about. General areas do not pinpoint the difficulty, but suggest that the entire reading process may be delayed.

1. *Mental Age.* The general problem may be related to the child's mental age or capacity, in which case the problem is not likely a remedial one, per se. The child who reads a few years below his grade level is not considered to have a reading disability if he is functioning at a level appropriate for his mental age.

2. *Verbal Intelligence.* Children from bilingual or disadvantaged backgrounds may have a normal potential, but test lower on verbal abstractions, vocabulary, reasoning, etc. When there is a wide discrepancy between verbal and performance areas on a test such as the Wechsler scale, the accompanying reading disability is normally one of a general, rather than a specific nature.

3. *Rate of Maturation.* A primary child may be late maturing, and may be reading below expectancy because of the maturational factors which delay the various hand-eye, visual, or perceptual abilities needed for complex skill of reading.

In each of the three areas listed above, the problem is one that may hopefully be expected to correct itself with time (maturity) and appropriate experiences (verbal abilities).

Standardized Tests for General Reading Ability

Most group achievement tests will give a level of general reading abiltiy at the various grade-levels (Lee-Clark, Metropolitan, etc., at the pre-literate to primary; Stanford Achievement Test, Iowa, Survey of Primary Reading Development, Gates Reading Survey, etc. at the elementary level and above).

The pupil's teacher, by general daily observation, can usually assess the child's general reading disability, and can give a fairly valid estimate of the pupil's grade placement in reading.

Individual standardized tests such as the Gray, Gilmore, Durrell, Monroe, or Gates can measure general oral reading speed, errors, or comprehension. The Wide Range Achievement Test (WRAT), though admittedly measuring only sight reading vocabulary, also gives a surprisingly accurate grade placement equivalent of a pupil's reading level.

Remediation of Specific Reading Problem Areas

(The following tasks and sample exercises should, of course, be varied according to the level of the child).

Sight Reading Vocabulary

1. Several wordlists can provide words for the child to learn; the better-known include the Dolch, Thorndike, and WRAT.

2. The child may need books and workbooks at a level at least 2 years below his instructional level, in order to establish a foundation of basic sight words.

3. The teacher can prepare illustrated exercises with simple multiple-choice answers, in which the pupil circles the correct word. (The dog ran into the..........................stove, yard, hat).

4. Exercises such as: Circle the things that fly: dog, cat, bird, chicken, horse, man, bat.

5. Use flash cards, gradually increasing the speed, and using words which are simple enough to encourage the child. The child is forced to develop a recognition of the word at sight, instead of analyzing the word formation.

6. Bulletin boards in the classroom may be constructed which contain words frequently missed by children, such as prepositions, pronouns, etc.

7. Word games may also be developed by the teacher for use by two or more children.

8. Children may be encouraged to develop "dictionaries" of words they frequently forget.

9. Tachistoscope exercises or programmed texts may be purchased to assist in the development of a child's sight vocabulary.

10. In cases of extreme disability, have the child dictate a simple, short story. The teacher prints the words the child has dictated and has the child "read" the words back (the child's memory is a help in this case). The words are then cut up and rearranged, so that the child gradually learns the words out of context.

11. The material must be interesting, presented in short sessions, and reinforcing to the child's feelings of progress. The teacher must not try to cover too much, and must not be overly encouraged by initial successes, lest he assume that the child has mastered the material too quickly.

Comprehension

1. Comprehension is a major purpose of reading. The child may have a sight vocabulary and a sense of phonics, but he still needs to comprehend what he has read, whether he is reading merely for pleasure or for information. Since comprehension is related to word-meaning skills, practice in the latter also aids comprehension.

2. Increase the child's vocabulary through experiences, then through meaningful discussion connected with the experiences. The experiences can be real (field trips, family outings, etc.) or vicarious (films, records, etc.), but they must have meaning for the child.

3. Gradually expand word-meaning into paragraph-meaning, or to thought-meaning of a larger idea (page or chapter). Comprehension is expanded as the word-meaning concept is expanded into larger units.

4. Most teacher instruction manuals and work-books contain a variety of further exercises for developing reading comprehension.

Word-meaning

1. Word-meaning skills are closely related to reading comprehension, and help in one also affects the other. The difficulty a child might have in attaching meaning to words is often found to be related to his oral pronunciation. Training and example should be carefully provided by the teacher.

2. Use visual association so that the child can picture the object or act depicted by the word (run, fall, rough, large).

3. Give practice in synonyms and antonyms. (The teacher gives a word; the student repeats with a word meaning the same thing, or the opposite thing. (Rough — smooth, large — small, etc.; ship — boat, automobile — car, etc.)

4. Provide picture clues for words, in which the picture depicts either a process or an object.

5. Gradually include words which emphasize starting consonants, vowels, blends, hard versus soft consonants, etc.

The "Over-phonetic" Reader

1. Use flash cards or a tachistoscope to encourage the child to recognize the whole word and speak it, without giving him time to go through the long analytical process of making the starting and subsequent sounds.

2. Teach the child to look for the root of the more complex words and for the prefix or suffix. This offers a quicker meaning to the reader than phoneticizing the word.

The Slow Reader

1. The passages the child is to read should be easy, short, and of interest to him. They should not be considered by the child as reading comprehension drills.

2. The child should be told that speed is the object and will be the goal expected. The purpose is for the child to learn to read as *fast* as he can with comprehension. This makes the identification of faulty habits appear more easily (finger-pointing, lip or mouth movements, excessive head movements, etc.), so that the faulty habits can be worked on. These habits can usually be frankly discussed with the child, and are rarely threatening to him.

3. The speed drills should be short, should be spread through the day, and the purpose made clear to the child. A progress chart, stop watch, etc., usually aid motivation.

Vocabulary Building

There is no substitute for experiential background and wide reading for building a child's vocabulary. There are, however, some classroom exercises which can be used toward this end.

1. Encourage the children to ask about new words, or words they do not fully understand. The teacher, too, should show curiosity about new or different words. The contagion of this inquisitive attitude can vitally affect the child's attitude toward learning about new or unusual words.

2. Put these words on the board, and find ways to encourage their use.

3. Keep the curriculum enriched, so that the children have materials to discuss and to think about. Keep magazines and books available, and encourage the children to refer to them. Make reference to them whenever possible.

4. Use new words in tests the teacher constructs. Give oral tests covering new words and their use, using them in sentences and discussing their meanings.

5. Be sure to use the words in context, rather than in isolation.

6. Always place the emphasis on meaning, rather than on recognition of the mechanics (pronunciation, spelling, etc.) of the word.

7. Encourage the children to make up and to use lists of new words they have learned to use.

8. Make an effort to see that the children look up an unknown word instantly, rather than waiting until a later time.

9. Have drills or games in finding synonyms or antonyms for words or phrases.

10. In the upper grades, allow time for word study with regard to roots, prefixes, and suffixes.

11. Encourage activities such as crossword puzzles, anagrams, etc.

SPELLING

Spelling

There are enough good standardized tests of spelling, based on national norms, for the teacher to easily and objectively identify a child with poor spelling and to locate the nature of the child's difficulty. These include, among others, the Stanford Achievement Test, Gates-Russell Diagnostic Spelling Tests, and Spache Spelling Errors Test. The Spelling Section of the WRAT also gives a quick grade-placement for the child.

Spache lists the major types of errors in spelling as: additions, omissions (of a single word or a syllable), transpositions (reversal of letters), and phonetic and nonphonetic substitutions. By examining the particular type of spelling difficulty from Spache's categories, the teacher can find the area(s) of spelling which most need help.

The use of spelling "rules" has been controversial, because of the frequent exceptions to the rule; however, the use of the rules for the poor speller usually offers more help than hindrance. Some of the better-known rules are:

1. "i" before "e" except after "c" (believe, receive).

2. "q" is always followed by "u".

3. The final 'y' on a noun becomes "ies" when plural (penny, pennies).

4. When a word ends in a silent "e" (quake), the "e" is dropped when a suffix is added (quaking).

5. Proper nouns and names always begin with a capital letter, (John, New York).

The teacher can easily prepare spelling tests, based on these and other rules, which are appropriate for the pupil's grade level or equivalent grade-placement. The pupil's study habits can also provide a clue (vision, handwriting, attitude, perceptual difficulties, etc.), and can provide a basis for individual remediation by the teacher or teacher-aide. The poor speller often has related difficulties involving his handwriting, reading, study habits, attitude, self-concept, etc. A pupil's habit of writing a word before he spells it orally is not considered bad practice.

Remediation of Poor Spelling

Happily, the remediation of most subject-matter areas also provides remediation for others. The same is especially true in spelling. Remedial reading, for example, often provides assistance for poor spelling.

1. The first step is an examination for, and possible elimination of, the intellectual and physical factors which are frequently associated with spelling disability. These include such things as the child's vision, hearing, speech, neurological dysfunction, and intelligence.

2. The types of errors made in speaking are also usually made in spelling (omissions, additions, substitutions of sounds, etc.). It has been found that speech therapy involving phonetic speech is directly related to improvement in spelling skills.

3. Improvement in handwriting is frequently accompanied by improvement in spelling. The fact that a child may write many illegible letters (q, p, o, a, etc.) also tends to make him perceive the letters in that manner. Further, many poor spellers, children and adults alike, either deliberately or subconsciously often write badly to conceal their spelling disability.

4. One's study habits and attitudes offer such a variety of individual differences that no one particular method of attack is best for all. As in reading, one's attitude toward spelling is as important as the method of study used. Dictionary usage, self-check, self-drill, etc., are valuable if the pupil is motivated, but relatively useless if he is not. Any method the teacher can devise by which the pupil can check himself is helpful. The teacher must make sure that the child is attempt-

ing words within his range of difficulty. It is better to have short, easy lists, gradually adding harder words as the pupil improves.

5. Remedial reading games have almost equal value for spelling. The games are adapted, of course, to the child's level, and can be tailor-made versions of anagrams, picture games, rhyming games, word puzzles, etc.

ARITHMETIC

Arithmetic

Generally, the most effective diagnosis of arithmetical difficulties is through the use of standardized tests, such as the California Achievement Test (Arithmetic section), Stanford Achievement Test, Iowa Every Pupil Test, etc. The Arithmetic section of the WRAT can indicate the grade level at which a pupil is working, and can also suggest gross types of errors. When standardized tests are not available, the teacher can usually easily construct a test from arithmetic texts at the respective grade level, and can group the test items as to subareas (addition, subtraction, multiplication, division, fractions, decimals, percentages, thought problems, arithmetic reasoning, etc.).

The teacher must make certain the pupil's difficulties are actually arithmetical, rather than problems relating to reading. Poor readers tend to achieve poorly on thought-process problems which involve reading instructions or concepts. Again, the reader is referred to Brueckner & Bond for a detailed analysis involving problem-solving and quantitative thinking in arithmetic, and to their chapter on remedial procedures for specific as well as general difficulties in arithmetic.

More often than not, a pupil's difficulties in arithmetic, as in reading, are complex, involving a combination of many of the factors, such as a fear of the subject, a particular skill missed in the current or preceding year, low level of intellectual functioning, delayed maturation, poor study habits, parental pressures, etc. Indeed, many pupils have difficulties with arithmetic because of a poor emotional "set", which may have been instilled by the parents, one of whom also had "trouble" with arithmetic.

HANDWRITING

Handwriting

Unlike reading, spelling, or arithmetic, it is more difficult to establish objective grade-level norms for a skill such as handwriting. There are, however, various levels of expected accomplishment, beginning with the 3-year level Binet drawing of a circle. At this level, crayons and coloring books take on a new meaning, and an adequate background here can often avoid future handwriting difficulties. First graders who are unable to print their first names or to print letters of the alphabet may be said to be possible eventual handwriting disability cases. First or second graders who are unable to use manuscript writing legibly are usually unable to learn cursive writing at the third grade level, or to enter into the developmental handwriting instruction of the middle-elementary grades.

The diagnosis of handwriting difficulties, as such, must be made by an individual teacher evaluation. There are various handwriting scales (Ayers, Minneapolis, Thorndike, etc.) which are relevant only in the upper grades. The major causes of faulty handwriting may be listed as physical (immaturity, readiness, visual, perceptual, neurological, intellectual) or as school-oriented problems, involving the school's failure to provide adequate instruction, or an overemphasis on rigid writing exercises. The latter is very rare.

Remediation

As with reading, remedial handwriting involves the same general techniques as used with general handwriting (nonremedial) instruction, though more attention is given to the specific problems found in the pupil's writing. Ellen Nystrom lists eight specific recommendations for improving handwriting in elementary school pupils:

1. Pressure of the pen or pencil must be light. Then pen should not be held down with the forefinger. The pen should not be held in a vertical position, but at about a 45 degree angle. The weight of the writing hand should be supported largely by the nails of the fourth and fifth fingers.

2. Irregular size is usually caused by holding the pen too straight. Writing too large can be caused from using too much arm movement, while writing too small is from using the fingers only. If

the thumb is bent directly into the pen, the correct amount of finger movement is permitted. Again, the size is more apt to be proper if the nails of the fourth and fifth fingers largely support the weight of the hand.

3. Irregular slant in writing is often the result of an incorrect slant of the paper, or caused from the habit of writing toward the right elbow (if the student is right handed).

4. Irregular spacing of letters is often caused by an improper slant of the letters, with crowded letters caused by too much slant, and diffused or scattered letters caused by too little slant. Attention must be given to making the upward curve of the letters in the standard slant.

5. All the letters of the alphabet except a, o, d, g, q, and e begin on the line. The upward slant for the ending letters should come up as high as the height of the small letters; thus, the beginning and ending strokes become an important factor in the remediation of handwriting.

6. The beginning and ending strokes also affect the crowding or scattering in the spacing of words. The beginning stroke of the new word should come just after the finishing stroke of the previous word. This avoids the problem of word-crowding. Allow an imaginary slant space for words beginning with a, o, d, g, q, and c.

7. The problem of alignment can be corrected when the paper is held properly and adjusted to the left frequently, so as to keep the writing directly within the line of vision. Poor alignment is caused by not shifting the paper often enough. When the paper is slanted too much the student tends to write below the line.

8. The form of the letters is related to the pupil's sense of rhythm. This may be helped by counting, in the early stage of remediation. Developing a flowing, rhythmic feel in writing decreases problems of size, slant, and spacing, and is perhaps the end result of teaching remedial handwriting.

References

Anderson, P., *Resource Materials for Teachers of Spelling,* Minneapolis, Burgess, 1959.

Ashlock, P. and Stephen, A., *Educational Therapy in the Elementary School,* Springfield, Ill., Charles Thomas, 1966.

Austin, M., Bush, L., and Heubner, M., *Reading Evaluation, Appraisal Techniques for School and Classroom,* New York, Ronald, 1961.

Bond, G. and Tinker, M., *Reading Difficulties: Their Diagnosis and Correction,* New York, Appleton-Century-Crofts, 1957.

Brownell, M., "Arithmetic in 1970," *The National Elementary Principal,* 1959.

Brueckner, L. and Bond, G., *The Diagnosis and Treatment of Learning Difficulties,* New York, Appleton-Century-Crofts, 1955.

Brueckner, L. and Grossnickle, F., *Making Arithmetic Meaningful,* Philadelphia, Winston, 1953.

Fernald, G., *Remedial Techniques in Basic School Subjects,* New York, McGraw-Hill, 1943.

Fitzgerald, J., *The Teaching of Spelling,* Milwaukee, Bruce, 1951.

Jastak, J. and Jastak, S., *WRAT Manual,* Wilmington, Guidance Associates, 1965.

Kottmeyer, W., *Teacher's Guide for Remedial Reading,* St. Louis, Webster, 1959.

Myers, P. and Hammill, D., *Methods for Learning Disorders,* New York, Wiley and Sons, 1969.

Nystrom, E., *Remedial Handwriting,* Minneapolis School Bulletin.

Otto, W. and McMenemy, R., *Corrective and Remedial Teaching,* New York, Houghton-Mifflin, 1966.

Peter, L., *Prescriptive Teaching,* New York, McGraw-Hill, 1965.

Smith, R., *Teacher Diagnosis of Educational Difficulties,* Columbus, O., Merrill, 1969.

4. Remedial Suggestions for Students with Varying Disabilities

A common concern of teachers regarding school psychologists is that, though they can select the appropriate test battery, diagnose a learning disorder in a child, and interpret the findings to the teacher or parent, often they cannot suggest to the teacher what can actually be done for the child in the classroom. Perhaps this is because we, as psychologists, have chosen to identify ourselves with other aspects of the profession, or perhaps it is simply that *we do not know* what to tell the teacher.

There is a definite trend, and a healthy one, as far as the optimal functioning of the school psychologist is concerned, for the recommendations to be prescriptive, practical, and specific for classroom application. It is with this in mind that the recommendations in this chapter have been made as basic and usable as possible for the remediation of the various disabilities. They have been listed by grade level and by the nature of the disability, such as visual, auditory, motor, articulation, or language.

Using instruments such as the Wechsler Scales, Stanford-Binet, Frostig, ITPA, etc., the psychologist may pinpoint areas of disability, and develop corresponding remediation techniques. Most of the following suggestions are merely "starting points," and should be adapted by the psychologist and teacher to meet the particular pupil and the classroom situation.

The teacher's readiness and willingness to accept such suggestions are, of course, prerequisites to successful implementation.

PRIMARY (Visual)

Primary Level

Suggestions for Primary Pupils Making Low Scores on Visual Tests

1. Place approximately 10 common articles (pencil, eraser, ball, paper clip, etc.) on a table in the front of the room; tell the children they are to look at the articles for a specified time (e.g., 10 to 15 seconds) and return to their seats. Beginning with the less able students, the teacher asks the children to name all the objects they can remember.

2. Ask the children to watch for common objects during the day, to be remembered the following day. Questions might include, "What color is on top of a traffic light?" "When a bird hops, does he hop with one foot, or on both feet together?" "On which side of a man's hat is the little bow?" "Which color of the stripe is on top of the American flag?"

3. Give incomplete pictures, on which the missing part is to be drawn.

4. Learn numerals 1 to 10 by writing in the air, in sand, and/or on paper, with the use of rhymes.

5. Put labels on most objects in the room. Have the children read the labels to complete the visual sentences the teacher reads. Use tracing and sound combination before attempting only visual memory of words.

6. The "touch game." The first player (one with lesser ability) touches an object and names it. The second player touches and names the same object and adds another to it. Keep increasing players and objects to be remembered.

7. Have a craft lesson with pictured instructions. Have the children study the pictures, then proceed to construct the object by recalling the instruction sequence.

8. Have the children follow the movements the teacher makes on the board without moving their heads.

9. Have the children look at a page in a catalogue or picture dictionary and try to recall the pictures seen.

10. Use a kinesthetic approach by having the children actually feel the shape of letters, words, numerals, etc. The shapes can be cut from sandpaper. The children trace the shape with their fingers, and; at the same time, repeat the name of what is being traced.

11. Similarities. Show two or more dissimilar objects to the children, and have them find ways in which they are alike.

12. Sequencing. Cut up cartoon pictures, and place them out of order. The children are to assemble them in the correct order.

13. Matching. Use any objects, such as blocks, colored marbles, etc., to reproduce similar designs.

14. Completion. The teacher presents pictures (hand drawn), and asks children to find the missing part.

15. Object assembly. Have the children assemble objects on the basis of form, or cut up pictures to use as jigsaw puzzles.

16. Use copies of *Child Life* or *Highlights for Children* to have the children find the pictures "hidden within" the magazine pictures.

PRIMARY (Auditory)

Suggestions for Primary Pupils Making Low Scores on Auditory Tests

1. Have the children reproduce various patterns of sounds made by the teacher (e.g., pencil tapping certain rhythmic patterns). The teacher claps out the number of syllables in the children's names, and the children repeat. Then do the same for cities, familiar long words, etc.

2. Have the children close their eyes and listen for as many sounds as they can hear. Have them tell what they are when their eyes are open.

3. Use bells of different pitch. Have the children respond by moving up for a high pitch and down for a low pitch.

4. Use a word orally, then have the children find it on a page.

5. Give the children practice in discriminating similar sounds, as in the Wepman Auditory Discrimination Test.

6. Make different sounds on tape from normal daily living (running water, doorbell, footsteps, etc.), and have children say what the sounds are. Context clues are important for the child with poor auditory discrimination.

7. Give the class (orally) several words with the opening consonant omitted. Have the children repeat the word as it should be (—eanut, —og, —utter, —octor, etc.).

8. Have blindfolded children identify others in class by their voices. Have them identify room sounds, such as tearing paper, typewriter, etc.

9. Use a tape recorder to give directions to the children. Gradually increase the length and complexity of the instructions.

10. Use sharing to have the children recall what the other children have said.

11. Using the Dolch cards, have the children collect all the cards they can name.

12. Have children repeat digits.

13. Tell stories, using sequence cards. Then have the children repeat the story with the use of the cards.

14. Play the whispering game, telling a story to a child, and having him whisper it to the child next to him, on to the next, and so on. When the story has gone around the group, have the last child tell the story he has heard.

PRIMARY (Motor)

Suggestions for Primary Pupils Making Low Scores on Motor Tests

1. Use dot-to-dot or number-to-number pictures.

2. Make class booklets of cloth with buttons and button holes, zippers, ribbons to be tied, hooks and eyes to open and close, etc.

3. Form objects, letters, numbers, etc. of clay.

4. Construct an obstacle race in which children must go over, under, and around obstacles.

5. Have the children teach a skill or game using only motion and gestures.

6. Use fine motor games, such as jacks, or relay races while carrying an object on a spoon, knife, etc.

7. Have the children prepare refreshments for school snack time, pouring Kool-Ade or milk, spreading peanut butter, etc.

8. Have the children make collages with cut-out pictures, letters, words, shells, beads, etc. Let the children use the typewriter to help in coordination, sequencing, and rhythmic hand-eye movements.

9. Develop coordination through the use of bean-bags, bead-stringing, skipping, block transfer, throwing, catching, etc.

10. Use exercises such as toe-touching, sit-ups, standing broad jump, etc.

11. Develop balance by the use of rail boards, walking forward, backward, blindfolded, etc.

12. Use maze puzzles freely.

13. Have the children make dittos for the teacher.

14. Develop rhythm by having the children keep time to music with their hands or feet, marching, etc.

15. Have the children make wooden or cardboard puzzles, maps, jigsaw puzzles, etc.

16. (For kindergarten). Learning to write numbers by rhymes:
    1: A straight line like one is fun.
    2: Around and back on a railroad track, two, two, two.
    3: Around a tree and around a tree is three.
    4: Down and over and down some more, that's the way to make a four.
    5: Fat old five goes down and around. Put a flag on top and see what you've found.
    6: Down to a loop, a six rolls a hoop.
    7: Across the sky and down from heaven, that's the way to make a seven.
    8: Make an S but do not wait. Climb back up to make an eight.
    9: A loop and a line is nine.
    10: It's easy to make a one and an 0. It is all of your fingers, you know.

17. Draw or paint to music, encouraging the children to move smoothly with the music, and to paint as much as possible with a continuous line. This encourages smooth, rhythmic hand movements and coordinated eye movements.

PRIMARY (Articulation)

Suggestions for Primary Pupils Making Low Scores on Articulation Tests

1. Have the children imitate sounds made by various animals.

2. Make a tape of a child telling a story and play it back to him. Do this privately if the child's articulation is embarrassing to him.

3. Stand next to the child in front of a mirror. Have him copy the teacher's pronunciation of words, sounds, sentences, etc., and watch the teacher's mouth and tongue formation. Immediate feedback with visual reinforcement is necessary.

4. Encourage the child to speak slowly and exaggerate mouth movements. Eventually extend this to having him try to convey a thought by having others read his lips.

5. Hold a paper in front of the mouth when making sounds.

6. Do choral reading and assign individual dramatic solos.

7. Have the children (especially the ones who most need it) seated so they can see the teacher's lips.

8. (For Kindergarten or first grade). Have the children pretend the tongue is a broom, and sweep the roof, floors, and walls, giving exercise for the tongue.

9. Use a game called "tongue twister," using a blend such as "fl," with the children making up the verse, such as "the flat flower fell with a flop onto the floor." Have the children volunteer to say it fast, and encourage them to laugh at their mistakes, so that even those with obvious speech problems participate along with the group.

10. Louise Scott's book *Talking Time* (Webster 1951) contains many ways in which the primary school teacher can help correct faulty articulation and aid speech development. Part II of the book offers "Special Help for Special Sounds." Many remedial techniques are used; one of the most effective is classroom participation in stories and poems using particular sounds.

PRIMARY (Language)

Suggestions for Primary Pupils Making Low Scores on Language Tests

1. Show an interesting picture to the class. Through oral participation, encourage the children to make up different stories to go with the picture.

2. Borrow sets of reading readiness books, and have the children find as many "things" in a picture as possible. The children can learn to spell from the sounds, and the teacher can make a list of synonyms to go with the children's sounds. The children then use the teacher's list of synonyms to fill in the blanks in sentences written by the teacher about the picture. This can later be put on tape so the sentences can be heard.

3. Play the game of "opposites." The teacher says a word. The first child to name its opposite gets the word card, points, etc. This may also be extended to homonyms.

4. Read a story to the class. Have the children list all the action words in the story (running, jumping, coming, etc.).

5. Involve the children in analogy games, in which a sentence has to be completed, either by the child's supplying the correct word, or by choosing the correct word from several. (e.g., "You wash your face with a cloth; you clean your teeth with a _____?")

6. Play "Bingo" with words, numbers, etc.

7. Use practice telephones, learning procedures for properly placing various types of phone calls.

8. Teach the children to talk with gestures, such as, "It was a BIG house," spreading his arms to demonstrate "big."

9. Have the children describe each other, using as many descriptive adjectives as possible.

10. With the use of a flannel board, have the children use the same figures, but invent different stories from the figures.

ELEMENTARY (Visual)

Elementary Level

Suggestions for Elementary Pupils Making Low Scores on Visual Tests

1. Teach the children to focus their eyes while turning around. Full and half turns can be done while traveling toward an object at the other end of the room. Learning to turn without getting dizzy will usually motivate children to focus their eyes.

2. Use the "light" game. One child moves a flashlight beam toward various objects in the room. The children follow the light, then identify the patterns, objects, or shapes. A variation is the reproduction by the students of various designs shown by the light for a few seconds, training the pupils to quickly focus on the object.

3. To develop visual memory, have the child copy sequences of bead designs, dominoes, or assorted objects.

4. Show several objects to the children on cards, screen, etc., and ask them to repeat the sequence of the objects.

5. Give exercises, such as the Coding subtest on the WISC, which train the pupil to remember the correct symbol, rather than to look back to the key for help.

6. Using a Tachistoflasher, have the children copy words, forms, or phrases presented.

7. Draw a frame around a word such as "little." Have the children suggest other words which have a similar configuration.

ELEMENTARY (Auditory)

Suggestions for Elementary Pupils Who Make Low Scores on Auditory Tests

1. Read a short, interesting story to the pupils, having them repeat as many of the incidents to you as they can.

2. Play records such as "Peter and the Wolf," teaching the pupils to recognize the characters by the sound of a musical instrument.

3. Teach basic rhythms on a drum. Start with a simple 4/4 pattern which is easily followed, and gradually become more complex. Children who play or who have studied a rhythmic musical instrument rarely score low on auditory tests.

4. Use a tape recorder to reproduce various sounds from the environment (train, whistle, etc.). Ask the children to reproduce orally what they have heard, and to make up stories about what they have heard.

5. Have the children note similarities or differences in the initial consonants of pairs of words (e.g., the similarities in "can" and "cat," and the differences in "cat" and "bat").

6. Suggest three words, two of which rhyme. Ask the children to pick out the one that does not rhyme.

ELEMENTARY (Motor)

Suggestions for Elementary Pupils Who Make Low Scores on Motor Tests

1. Teach a child to express his feelings through body movements. There are basic techniques in creative dance which would not be difficult for the average teacher to learn and apply. Elementary age children easily become emotionally involved with the expression of their own body movements. With continued practice, much of the inhibitions soon leave, and the pupils gain freedom of movement.

2. Use "number" painting for pictures.

3. Make figurines, ashtrays, baskets, etc., as gifts for parents.

4. For the development of small motor skills, craft work such as metal tooling or model making is usually motivating.

5. The teacher can invent simple motor games that can be played in the classroom, on rainy days, etc. These can be patterned after musical chairs, eraser tag, etc.

6. Provide coloring books (at an appropriate level for elementary pupils). Learning to stay within lines is excellent motor practice.

7. A class project such as a large mosaic or mural, can be planned.

8. Have the class construct and exchange mazes, asking them to trace the maze to the goal. Details may be used to make the mazes more attractive or complex, to meet the needs of the pupils.

ELEMENTARY (Articulation)

Suggestions for Elementary Pupils Who Make Low Scores on Articulation Tests

1. Encourage the child to prepare a book with as many of the troublesome words and sounds as he and the teacher can think of. Each word entered in the book should be one that has become mastered in the process of entering it.

2. Using a mirror, the teacher says the sound which is of concern to the pupil. The child, with the use of the mirror, tries to make the sound, using the same mouth movements. A tape recording of the pupil's original sounds, followed by the new "learned" sound, can serve as a motivator.

3. R, s, ch, and sh are among the most common articulation problem sounds at the intermediate level. Using a vocabulary list from reading and spelling lessons, the teacher can compile a list of flash cards (two of each), and use them for students to play as rummy. The pupil can make pairs by asking for a word from other members of the group. The pupil who has the card must answer, using the word in a sentence. The game continues until one pupil has all (or most) of the cards.

4. Ideally, speech defects should be corrected before the child has begun reading, because infantile speech, substitutions, lisping, stuttering, etc., may interfere with later reading. The children might play "sound" games, identifying the kinds of sounds found in the environment. Most speech sounds are either "air sounds" or "vibrations." The child can be shown both, and helped to differentiate. An example is the use of an air pump and a rubber band, producing the "ah" and "oh" sounds as opposed to the "l," "m," and "n" sounds.

5. Have the children enact a short but meaningful scene with a theatrical stage setting. When promoted the right way, children can easily become "performers," and in their projection will strive to be better understood.

6. The teacher can identify for the children each sound of the language and relate it to a sound from the environment (e.g., "s" is a tire losing air, a whistling kettle, etc.).

ELEMENTARY (Language)

Suggestions for Elementary Pupils Making Low Scores on Language Tests

1. Make word games out of synonyms and antonyms. Develop sets of flash cards with the "opposite" card and a "similar" card.
2. The pupils can write the script for a play, puppet show, or TV script.
3. Encourage the use of student oral or written reports on their hobbies. If language is not fluent, encourage the use of props, such as the object itself (models, stamps, etc.).
4. The teacher provides the class with a topic sentence, from which the class makes up a story.
5. Have spontaneous "dramas," in which the students pretend they are involved in a situation which requires language (e.g., one is "accused" of stealing, is a "witness," and must "testify").
6. Discuss shades of meaning in synonyms, such as big and immense, tiny and small, etc. Have the children develop their own thesaurus. Have the pupils see how many synonyms they can find for certain words.
7. Encourage class sharing, especially when it is about family outings, hobbies, trips, etc., which represent pleasure for the child.

JUNIOR HIGH (Visual)

Junior High Level

Suggestions for Junior High Pupils Making Low Scores on Visual Tests

1. Make frequent use of such devices as the tachistoscope and flash cards. Pupils of this age are very competitive, but feel a sense of "adult" dignity not seen in the elementary pupil; thus, the elementary "fun and games" approach must now be avoided.
2. Give the group 15 to 20 seconds to study a picture, then allow 10 to 15 minutes to write all they can about it.
3. Use the controlled reader to develop left to right eye movement.
4. Use the blackboard often, keeping important information on the board and changing the contents daily.

JUNIOR HIGH (Auditory)

Suggestions for Junior High Pupils Making Low Scores on Auditory Tests

1. Have the pupil spell words from dictation in which only one phonetic element changes (e.g., it, fit, fist, mist, must, just, rest, best, bet, etc.).
2. Provide training in listening for specific consonant sounds, to instantly tell whether the sound is at the beginning, middle, or end. Give training in counting the number of syllables, for the accented syllable, the unaccented syllable, etc.
3. Encourage the use of the pronunciation key in the dictionary, exploring new or difficult words.
4. Make use of materials, such as the SRA Listening Exercises, "Listen and Read" tapes and workbooks, and story-question exercises, such as the Binet "Wet Fall."
5. Encourage the use of choral speaking.
6. Develop the practice of making important announcements only once, and in a relatively soft voice. The pupils must learn that the material will not be repeated, and that they must learn to pay close attention.

JUNIOR HIGH (Motor-Articulation)

Suggestions for Junior High Pupils Making Low Scores on Motor Tests

1. Make full use of school activities involving motor skills, such as physical education, making posters, paper-folding crafts (airplanes, birds, flowers, designs, etc.), knitting, sewing, cooking, shop, dancing, etc. The junior high pupils who is not adept in motor skills tends to avoid them and needs special encouragement to participate.
2. Encourage the pupil to develop his penmanship, giving him the rules, opportunity for practice, etc., and display work whenever possible.
3. Permit pupils to use fingers to underline words as they read.
4. Have the pupils construct, share, and work mazes, gradually increasing in difficulty.

Suggestions for Junior High Pupils Making Low Scores on Articulation Tests

1. Encourage lip reading (speech reading) by the students, who must learn the formation of letters and sounds visually. Students who can learn to lip read usually improve their own articulation skills.

2. Use tongue-twisters, such as "black bugs blood," "rubber baby buggy bumpers," etc.

3. Students sufficiently motivated can use the tape recorder by themselves, check their own improvement, identify their weak areas, etc.

4. Use choral speaking, class plays, word games, etc.

Suggestions for Junior High Pupils Making Low Scores on Language Tests

1. Use the many programmed materials for this age, such as Sullivan's Readers, English 2200, etc.

2. Over-pronounce spelling words. Read often to the class, encouraging the students to read and to write for pleasure. Encourage creative writing, class discussion, etc.

3. Demonstrate comparative adjectives (tall, taller, tallest), using objects. Use a word incorrectly in a sentence, and have the students identify the incorrect word.

HIGH SCHOOL (Visual)

High School Level

Suggestions for High School Students Making Low Scores on Visual Tests

1. Relate the remedial tasks to the student's interests and vocational plans. Have the students identify geometric objects (spheres, pyramids, cones, etc.) that become increasingly ambiguous to the point that they become objects of everyday use. Remediation at this level is usually at the student's own initiative, and can be approached frankly.

2. The student can make use of the various devices, such as the tachistoscope, flash cards, slides, etc., as are used in the military.

3. Provide experience for the student in learning to recognize words, phrases, etc., which are exposed for only 1 or 2 seconds. Visual acuity and reading speed and comprehension are related to the extent that the remediation of one also helps the other. The self-use of equipment such as the tachistoscope can gradually increase the student's visual recognition span to include longer phrases or sentences.

HIGH SCHOOL (Auditory-Motor)

Suggestions for High School Students Making Low Scores on Auditory Tests

1. Encourage enrollment (perhaps as an auditor, only) into a foreign language class. Ideally, the language should be one which could be of practical value to the student.

2. Train the student(s) to listen closely to instructions by giving them only once.

3. Many students at this level have improved their auditory skills with the use of a tape recorder and headset. They have trained themselves to hear something only once, then to write or say what they have heard. The level of volume can be gradually turned down, as the student learns to eliminate extraneous sounds or thoughts. Distracting stimuli (physical or emotional) are considered a major factor in auditory deficiency.

Suggestions for High School Students Making Low Scores on Motor Tests

1. If no reading difficulty is concommitant, concentrate on improving neuro-muscular coordination, beginning at an elementary level. Eye-hand coordination and fine, dexterous, manipulative movements of hands and fingers are particularly important in mechanical and clerical fields. Tasks can be related to occupations, and materials used should be familiar and of interest to the student (e.g., hand tools or business machines). Start with the simpler tasks, and gradually move to the more complex. Large muscle motor skills usually improve much more rapidly than the fine motor areas.

2. Encourage the use of hobbies which help to develop muscular coordination (athletics, auto repair, electronics, etc.).

HIGH SCHOOL (Articulation)

Suggestions for High School Students With Articulation Difficulties

1. Correction of articulation defects at this age becomes far more difficult, although the student's motivation can now become a key factor. Learning a foreign language can often help the student to concentrate on sounds or phrases he has

avoided in the past, especially when he attempts to imitate the inflections, accents, etc., of the new language. Many students who stutter in English do not have this problem in a new language; thus, their speech in English gradually improves.

2. Encourage the student to speak before the group, with an honest approach to the class. The peer influence at this level is usually an encouragement, rather than a deterrent to good speech. A group of students with articulation difficulties could form a "public speaking" class on a small basis, providing opportunity for them to evaluate each other. At this age level, self-consciousness is one of the greatest factors in overcoming articulation defects.

HIGH SCHOOL (Language)

Suggestions for High School Students Making Low Scores on Language Tests

1. Encourage the student toward independent reading, regardless of the literary value of the reading. Many students with this difficulty avoid reading because of vocabulary, language, or comprension problems. Even the worst "dime novels," while lacking in literary value, are full of vocabulary words in the context, and are not noted for poor grammar or usage. Oral or written book reports can be of value. There is a high correlation between articulation, reading, and language usage at this level.

5. Suggestions for Initial Handling of Typical Referrals

The school psychologist is generally not expected to clinically treat major behavior disorders in school pupils. Indeed, in many states such treatment is illegal. The psychologist's training has often not included depth therapy; further, the school is not a clinic, nor was it intended to be.

He is, however, expected to recognize the symptoms and understand the causes of common academic and behavior disorders, and to make recommendations toward initiating the alleviation of the problem. Many school psychologists find that they receive nearly as many referrals from the home as from the school; therefore, many of the following typical referrals include those commonly requested by parents, as well as by teachers or administrators.

The list of topics includes some of the most common referrals the school psychologist might expect, and a starting point in the management of the problem. The bibliography at the end of this chapter contains texts which treat the various disorders in greater detail. The psychologist might also do well to gradually accumulate lists of appropriate referral agencies for the treatment of disorders for which he feels the need for help.

ACCELERATION (SEE RETENTION)

Frequently a parent or a teacher will want a child to be considered for acceleration to a higher grade, because of his superior intellectual and/or academic ability. Generally, there is no special rule-of-thumb which applies to acceleration; rather, each case should be considered on its own merits.

Acceleration is generally inadvisable except in very special cases. Following is a list of the major factors which should be considered before the final decision is made, although none in themselves should constitute the entire case.

1. *C.A.* Children whose birthdate falls between early December and March or April are those who would nearly have been in a higher grade, had their birthday been earlier. Thus, a December or January birthdate could be considered as a "plus" factor in acceleration, an October or November birthday a consideration against it.

2. *I.Q.* Although the I.Q. score, itself, should not be a basis for acceleration, those being considered should certainly be above average in intelligence.

3. *Academic Ability.* Academic grade placement scores (group, such as the Stanford Achievement Test, California Achievement Test, Iowa, etc.; and, *individual,* such as the Wide Range Achievement, or teacher estimate) should place the child at or above the grade level for which he is being considered. Most important here are reading, language, and spelling. Arithmetic at the elementary level is not too often far above grade level, because specific skills involved may not yet have been covered in class. Reading comprehen-

sion is probably the best predictor of elementary school academic success.

4. *Peer Relationships.* If the child has grown up in the same neighborhood and has a close relationship with his chronological age peers, being singled out of the group for acceleration could pose social or emotional difficulties for the child.

5. *Siblings.* Does the child have a sibling in the grade to which consideration is being given? It would probably be damaging to the family structure if, for example, a third grader were accelerated to the fourth grade, where a sibling was enrolled, even if they were in separate rooms.

6. *Sex.* Because of the rate of maturation, a girl might generally be considered a better risk for acceleration than a boy. This of course does not rule out boys, but presents one further dimension to the problem.

7. *Physical and Emotional Maturity.* Will the child visually appear out of place in the new setting because of his physical size? More important, will the child *feel* out of place. Intramural sports, for example, and future classroom "romances" can be affected. If the child is not relatively secure emotionally, the move could prove harmful. Further, the school must consider whether the child is secure enough to handle the new social situation.

8. *Parental Attitude.* The schools have long known that unless the parents approve a move of this importance, the home climate and discussions can hurt the chances for success. More often than not, the parents are flattered that their child is considered for acceleration and whole-heartedly endorse the move, volunteering to help with the child's assignments until the child has caught up. Too often it is the parents, themselves, who initiate the proposal, stating that their child is "bored" with the easy work.

When all the factors are weighed, the person responsible for the proposed move considers the number of positive answers to the issues listed above, as opposed to the negative. The acceleration should be carefully explained to the child, that he is going to visit the room for a period of time to see if it seems to work out. The child is not "on trial," so to speak, but it should be made clear to the child that this period (of a month, or so) is a time for the school and the child, himself, to see if it was best to do this. There must be no feelings of failure if the child needs to be returned to the previous grade after this period.

AGGRESSIVE BEHAVIOR

Extreme aggressive behavior may be manifested through a physically aggressive act, or, when the act is restricted, through words, looks, or thoughts. It is often caused by the child's reactions to parental overindulgence, or, worse, the overprotection associated with parental rejection. It is also frequently caused by the child's reaction to the parents' unfair or severe physical punishment, or by the child's siding with one parent (usually the mother) in parent disputes or incompatibility. Aggressive behavior is worsened when the parents comply with the child's demands in an effort to avoid the behavior. Each successful experience on the part of the child tends to perpetuate the behavior. The overindulged child often tends to use this behavior at home, rather than with strangers.

The parents should not physically punish the child by using the same physical force they are trying to teach the child to avoid. They should wait until the behavior has subsided before any reasoning begins. Sometimes having the child with older or larger children is helpful. Opportunities for aggressive play activities such as running, hammering, pounding, etc. are helpful. The child also should be given increasing responsibility whenever possible. The child who sees himself as responsible for consistent routines tends to use aggressive behavior far less than the child who needs reminding to perform chores. When it is necessary to remove the child, it should be done without comment, and with as little aggression or restraint as possible on the part of the adult.

The home situation should be examined to determine whether the parents are unwittingly encouraging aggression by example or by inhibiting or intimidating the child.

ANXIETY

Every person will sometimes experience mild or acute anxiety reactions, some of which may become persistent or chronic. They are usually manifested in feelings of guilt, panic, fear, apprehension, or tension, and are frequently associated with an experience such as going to school or to the hospital. Chronic anxiety results from acute anxiety which has not been resolved, and is usually related to the repression of interpersonal problems, conflicts between sexual and aggressive drives, or the like.

Senn and Selnit advise the physician to use caution in lending a label such as "nervous" or "run-down" to the condition, which tends to minimize the emotional aspects. Though the symptoms need to be treated, the basic management must get at the source of the anxiety. The parents, as well as the child, need to be assured that the young body and mind are resilient, and that once insight by the child is gained into the source of the conflict (the cause), the anxiety (the symptom) gradually dissipates.

CHEATING

The chief concern here is not that the child has cheated, but why he feels the need to cheat, and whether it is an isolated or a regular practice. Most every person at one time or another has felt a need to cheat in order to ensure a better test paper. When it becomes an ongoing practice, however, it assumes another dimension. Some practical questions might pinpoint the reasons: Is the work too hard? Are home or school pressures too great? Are the pressures real or imagined? Is the child trying to compete with a more successful sibling? Are the child's own standards too high? Are the opportunities for cheating too easy at school? Do the parents place an undue emphasis on grades?

A confrontation, per se, could be damaging to the child. Rather, the child needs to know of the teacher's awareness of the problem, but the manner in which this is done is also important. The teacher or interviewer should privately talk with the child in an easy, helpful, and non-punitive manner. The child must not see himself labeled as a type, nor should he see implications that he is a habitual cheater. The child needs to see the adult as an interested person, eager to eliminate the causes of the cheating, and should be encouraged to freely discuss what he feels are the possible causative factors.

The parents should become involved only after the efforts by the school to correct the problem have failed.

COMPULSIVE TALKING

The practice of compulsive or incessant talking, usually found most in pre-school children, is not as undesirable as it is irritating to parents. It can be eased by the encouragement of outside interests, especially those involving physical activity. This habit in the school age child usually suggests a need for an examination of the emotional climate in the home, and a need to find ways to give the child recognition for more socially acceptable behavior.

Verville feels that the child who talks excessively has problems which are unresolved and which require solutions. She recommends that parents reserve time each day to spend with the child and that the child know that he will be carefully listened to at this time. The child should also be *required* to be quiet at certain times.

DAYDREAMING

Daydreaming is known by many names, and is common to all children and adults. It is far from undesirable, unless practiced to excess, as it offers time for imagination, planning, reverie, and escape. The peak of the habit usually comes during adolescence, when the child is confronted with conflicts concerning love, ambition, adulthood, etc.

Causes of excessive daydreaming include the following: children who must spend much time alone in their room; children who lead lonely and boring lives; children whose school work is too difficult for them; children who are able to function markedly above the level of the school work provided them; those who frequently meet with failure or frustration; those whose home life is not stimulating or interesting; the invalid; the only child.

The management of the problem is indicated only when there is evidence that the child daydreams to excess, to the extent that his school work or personal life is suffering. The treatment involves matching (as nearly as possible) the daydream. The child needs life to be more interesting, to have more companions, more social interchange, more involvement with others.

The parents must be made aware of the problem, and must help correct the causes which stem from the home. The school should consider the proper placement of the child in the room, group, or even grade. Often the child will divulge the contents of the daydreams, which tend to follow a certain theme and which indicate possibilities for solution.

DISCIPLINE (MANAGEMENT OF CLASSROOM BEHAVIOR)

Children are well aware when they have emotionally involved a teacher or parent through misbehaving, and are quick to respond in kind when the adult loses his poise. Many teachers have lost control of their entire class through losing emotional control over one student.

Dr. Winfield Wickham lists some practical techniques which should apply to most classroom disciplinary problems.

1. Enlist the child's cooperation. Get him to work with you toward a recognized acceptable goal. Make it a learning experience. Do not moralize or "harp."

2. Establish a routine, so that the mechanics and goals of adjustment and conforming become internalized as habits.

3. Cooperatively set up a clear, concise set of formalized rewards and penalties. These should be understandable to the child's level of maturity and agreed upon beforehand as fair and workable.

4. Our best discipline comes from example and imitation. Children are seldom original either in their conduct or misconduct.

5. A practical distinction must be made between needs and wants. One is never justified in restricting or depriving a child of his needs, but it is possible to set up a system depriving his wants. Try to help the child replace the undesirable behavior with something at least as satisfying.

DROPOUTS

There are any number of reasons high school pupils drop out of school, most of which are superficial. Generally, when the student sees that he is not succeeding or heading toward a meaningful goal, he often simply drops out. Problems related to dropping school are the following:

1. The child may feel the curriculum is meaningless to him.

2. Lower class and disadvantaged children often do not feel part of the program.

3. A lack of understanding as to just what an academic education is for.

4. Parents themselves may have been dropouts, and do not place a value on education.

5. School underachievement.

6. A lack of sense of purpose or personal responsibility.

7. Chances outside the school for vocational or personal success.

Of all the causes listed above, the last is believed to represent the best adjusted group of school dropouts, both personally and socially. The continuation high school has occasionally proved a fairly successful plan toward averting dropouts, but as our present high school is set up, little other than individual or family counseling has proved helpful. A special interest in school-related activities, such as athletics, pre-vocational training, etc., also helps.

DRUG ABUSE

The role of the counselor or psychologist with regard to drug abuse will vary according to the philosophy of the district as to whether there should be a referral, and whether the referral should be legal, administrative, medical, or parental. The counselor *does* need, however, to be aware of the general categories of drugs, and to recognize the most common symptoms of their use.

The drugs most commonly used by school-age youngsters are the hallucinogens (marijuana, LSD), stimulants ("Bennies," "Dexies," etc.), and depressants (various barbiturates). All are readily available on the street black market, and in small quantities are within the price range the adolescent can afford. Stimulants and depressants are usually easily obtained from the parent's medicine cabinet.

The clues to marijuana usage in the youngster include dilation of pupils and extreme sensitivity to light, impaired judgment and general disinhibition, a chronic bronchial cough, excessive desire for sweet foods and liquids, and excessive talking. The user of amphetamines usually manifests hyperactivity, restlessness, excessive talking and arguing, loss of appetite, sleeplessness, and disinhibited behavior.

DYSGRAPHIA

This disorder, involving writing difficulties such as mirror-writing, reversals, and writing upside down, though found in both sexes, is more prevalent in boys. The child's reading also usually includes similar or related errors. The causes include neurological disorders and the accompanying poor motor control, switching from left-to right-handedness, emotional involvement, mild mental retardation, and occasional careless early training and habits.

Retraining is now indicated, and should be done gradually and in a positive and encouraging manner. Attention should be given to such minor details as the manner in which the pencil is held, the slant and position of the paper, a slowed-down tempo of writing, proper arm movements, and to the older methods of handwriting, such as the Palmer method, which offers full arm and wrist practice in writing.

The feelings of accomplishment must be maintained, because the remediation of this difficulty often seems to the child to be a long and routine task. It involves simply a period of retraining, with orderly, periodic, purposeful drill, consisting of short practice sessions. As the child becomes aware that the difficult can be corrected through practice and through neuro-muscular training, he becomes more interested in continuing. The practice sessions must be short (5 to 10 minutes, depending on the child's age and level of frustration), frequent (at least daily, hopefully, several short periods each day), supervised (to avoid reverting to former incorrect habits), and reinforcing.

DYSLEXIA

Dyslexia, often called word-blindness, reading retardation, reading disability, alexia, etc., is an inability to deal effectively with printed symbols. It is often neurologic in origin, but may also be psychological. Common among retardates, it is difficult to diagnose in this group because of the overall low academic achievement level of the retarded. A remedial reading program is indicated (with the normal as well as the retarded) if the elementary child reads or spells 2 years or more below his mental age or grade level. Indeed, without remediation, these children tend to remain dyslexic.

The dyslexic child frequently shows a wide scatter in his intelligence test profile, and is often misplaced in school because of the effect dyslexia has upon his total IQ score. The test profile often reveals strengths which represent the child's best means of learning, and through which remediation can be most effective.

Frequently even though the reading level might improve, the dyslexic child tends to be nonphonetic, and to remain a poor speller. (Reading, a more receptive skill, is more easily improved than spelling, which the child must independently *produce*.) The attention is often directed toward the gradual phonetic approach to reading (see Chapter 3, Reading).

Most educators agree that the use of as many approaches as feasible (visual, auditory, kinesthetic, tactile) is best. Orton recommends the following approach: (1) progressing from small units the child can handle through orderly simple steps to the more complex units. (2)) Using as many sensory pathways as possible simultaneously (e.g., the child verbalizes as he traces a letter, looks and points to it as he hears it read, etc. Severe cases need referral to a clinic, for most schools are not equipped to treat the "totally illiterate" dyslexic.

EATING HABITS

Mothers are prone to worry more than fathers over whether the child eats his food, eats enough, eats only certain foods, etc. Interestingly, it is usually this worry, itself, which perpetuates a child's unwillingness to eat without urging.

The solution is far easier than most parents would imagine, but is often avoided because it involves consistency and objectivity by the parents. Once a medical evaluation has shown there to be nothing physically wrong which is contributing to the problem, a simple routine can virtually eliminate the problem of a child's not eating his food without urging.

1. A child *will* eat if he is hungry, and if there are no secondary gains via attention or parental involvement if he does *not* eat. The refusal of the parent to show concern is the first and most important step in the correction of the problem. Far too often, the mealtime becomes a time of pleading, threatening, lectures, etc., rather than a pleasurable period to both parents and siblings.

2. When the parents have completed their dinner, and an adequate time is allotted the child to finish, the meal and dishes are quietly removed from the table, without comment by the parent. This is the most difficult task for the parent, as many feel a need for an "I told you I'd take it away if you didn't eat" remark. This should in no way be punitive, or it easily loses its effect, becoming a contest which the child can usually win.

3. Do not let the child eat between meals or before bed.

4. Remain indifferent. It must not appear to matter whether the child eats or not. No hungry, healthy child will starve himself, unless the secondary gains of prodding, cajoling, parental nervousness, etc., are equally desirable for the child.

5. Call the child to dinner only once. Children who are aware of the parents' concern over their eating habits tend to delay coming to the table. The child soons learns that if the family will eat without him and the table is quietly cleared when the prescribed time is over, it is in his best interest to come quickly.

This sounds over-simplified, but case studies have shown that, once the physical aspects have been ruled out, the problem of eating has been one of our most needless concerns.

ENURESIS

A child may be called enuretic if he is unable to remain dry at night after age 3. This disorder is found in both sexes, but is far more prevalent in boys. There is considerable evidence that the condition is contributed to by hereditary factors, although if the child has stopped bed-wetting by age 6 to 8, he rarely returns to the practice.

A medical evaluation should be obtained for the child. Occasionally a urinalysis will reveal contributing medical factors such as from white blood cells. Medication such as Impiramine has been found helpful. Another current practice is the use of a pad which electrically activates a bell when set, thus alerting the child when he starts to bed-wet. The child's awareness that he is becoming able to either control the habit, or is at least aware of when he starts, is a considerable force in the cure.

Counseling with the child should always be positive, encouraging, and geared toward building his self-confidence and hope. Counseling with the parents should be toward ridding them of feelings of guilt for having helped bring on the condition in their child. They need to be reminded that the causes are considered to be more hereditary than psychological, and that once begun, nervous tensions on the part of the child *or* parent only accentuate the problem (Bakwin and Bakwin).

EYE EXERCISES (OCULAR TRAINING)

Optometrists familiar with perceptual difficulties have frequently been referred to as reading disability cases, and have often prescribed a series of ocular exercises designed to improve eye-muscle coordination ability. The child is also trained in the ability to use both hands simultaneously in drawing prescribed circles, arcs, and figures, toward improving hand-eye coordination and perceptual abilities.

Jastak, Money, and others feel that ocular defects, per se, are only a negligible factor in dyslexia, and that such exercises, designed to improve reading, are based more on a fad than on scientific evidence.

EYE PREFERENCE

Eye preference, or eyedness, refers to the dominant or habitually used eye in sighting. To determine the eye of preference in a child, he may be asked to sight through a small hole in a piece of paper. It is generally considered that the preferred eye matches the dominant hand, so that normally the right-eyed child is also right-handed. Some disagree with this, stating that it does not adequately account for right-eyed, left-handed people. The so-called mixed dominance has been considered a possible factor in reading difficulties. Though eye preference is even more difficult to change than handedness, and most authorities agree that it should not be changed, many have gradually trained themselves to change the eye dominance by repeatedly using it for sighting.

HAND PREFERENCE

Hand preference in today's society generally holds little interest for parents. Studies suggest that families in which one of the parents is left-handed tend to have more concern about helping their child become right-handed, having apparently felt left-handedness to be a problem. Actually, the incidence of right-handedness *is* greater in these families. Families with right handed parents have no great interest in hand preference, and the normal ratio of about 7% persists.

Although there is dispute as to the cause of hand preference (Gesell considers its hereditary, Blau feels it is cultural), it is generally believed that handing an infant objects to his right hand, or making it convenient for him to use his right hand during his first year of life will help to establish the hemispherical dominance. Once the hand preference has been established by the infant, no attempt should be made to change it.

HOMOSEXUAL TENDENCIES

Homosexual activity in childhood is frequently engaged in by boys through mutual masturbation, although what is considered a consistent homosexual pattern usually does not become established until the late teens. The effeminate boy with an excessive desire for affection and reassurance usually begins the activity earlier than the more masculine boy and tends to continue in his passive role. Some researchers suggest that homosexual children tend to imitate an admired homosexual parent or friend, or to have a delayed or thwarted identification with an adult of the same sex.

Often, the attachment is formed with a man or older boy the child admires at a time the boy needs assurance and support, and the relationship is permitted by the boy because of his admiration for the person. In these cases, the attachment usually dissolves when the older person moves from the area, and does not usually reappear unless another similar person is available when the boy is vulnerable. The practice, initially distasteful and guilt-laden for the boy, eventually becomes pleasurable.

An excessively strong mother-son relationship is also considered a factor in homosexuality. The mother, usually unconsciously, over-protects him, accompanies him, etc. Typically, the father-son relationship is weak, and the father himself is generally passive or impotent.

A changed environment is basic in helping the young homosexual. The boy must not find himself surrounded by homosexuals or opportunities. A busy, active life with masculine interests and hobbies is desirable. A natural, but not forced, social relationship with the opposite sex must be available. An admired masculine male identification is desirable.

The boy must be made to know that there are no physical, genetic, or glandular causes for this behavior, and that he is not destined to this because of something about his body. His feelings of guilt and inadequacy can often be resolved by a frank discussion. The earlier in the boy's development this can happen, the greater the chances for complete recovery.

HYPERACTIVITY (HYPERKINESIS)

Hyperactivity, distractibility, or short attention span are often found in children with emotional or neurological involvement. The greatest incidence is among boys, aged pre-school to adolescence. This "driven" behavior often dissipates by the early teen years.

The child seems unable to contain himself; he is so distractible that he darts about, starts but does not finish things, cries easily, and because he is unable to sit for prolonged periods of time, poses a problem to the school as well as to his parents, both of whom tend to blame the child for his "misbehavior." Because the multiple stimuli make the condition usually more pronounced at school, parents often tend to blame the school for not handling the child properly.

The physical evaluation and the resulting medical control has been found helpful in many cases; indeed, many such children would be unable to stay in school without medication. The child should be given school assignments of such length that they can more easily be completed. His condition should be recognized by the teacher to the extent that he might be given tasks such as passing out papers, sharpening pencils, etc., which permit him to be out of his seat more often than usual. In more severe cases, the symptoms might suggest consideration for placement in an EH or learning disability group.

Two major classes of drugs are often used in the treatment of hyperkinesis:

1. The sympathomimetic amines, which, though actually stimulants, often tend to show beneficial results in hyperactive children. The two most widely used drugs in this category are dextro-amphetamine and methylphemidate, the latter being the more common.

2. The phenothiazines (tranquilizers). The two most preferred drugs in this category seem to be chlorpromazine and thioridazine.

Physicians report that tranquilizers slow down hyperkinetic children more predictably than the sympathomimetic amines, but the quality of the resulting behavior is seldom as good (Dr. Harold Burks, in the Los Angeles County Research and P.P.S. Letter, March, 1970).

HYPOCHONDRIASIS

This preoccupation with body fatigue and illnesses is common among adolescents and adults, but rare among young children. The actual diagnosis of hypochondriasis is usually made when the physician is unable to find any physical disease present. The patient usually has symptoms of anxieties and phobias, which the child interprets as physical disease (e.g., hyperventilation, nervousness, heart palpitations, constipation, insomnia, tension headaches, etc.).

Though physicians frequently, and often successfully, prescribe sedatives or tranquilizers, they sometimes do not have or take time to take advantage of the person's willingness to talk about his problems. The hypochondriac is usually eager to discuss his ailments, thus providing a ready avenue for therapy not found in many other emotional disorders. Senn and Selnit advise that once the physician has ruled out physical disease he must avoid overtreatment, lest the child or adolescent cling to this behavior which has brought him gratification. As an adult, the hypochrondriac tends to resort to chronic invalidism as a means of coping with adult problems. Childhood hypochondriasis is often related to hypochondriacal parents, more often the mother. Children often simulate the ailments of the parents. Outside activities are vital. These might include scouting, hobbies, athletics, church, clubs, etc. The more physical the activity, the sooner the child will see himself as physically fit.

IDIOGLOSSIA

Idioglossia refers to a condition in which the child's speech is not readily understood by an adult. The condition, not to be confused with delayed speech development associated with mental retardation, is usually characterized by frequent reversals, the use of similar or rhyming starting or ending sounds, or it may be an "original" language. The condition is found mostly among children left together a great deal, twins, families with several children of near the same age, and among children with delayed speech or audiological difficulties. It is often inadvertently encouraged by parents (usually mothers) who understand and imitate the language pattern with their child. The habit, unless physically induced, normally dissipates on its own with maturity and the development of outside interests.

IMAGINARY PLAYMATES

This is a common practice among most children of pre-school age, and is more common among girls than boys. The child usually treats his imaginary playmate very well, and the social graces are common among the two. The relationship generally seems to be happy and constructive, and merely suggests that the child has devised a means to combat loneliness or boredom. It might also suggest that the child is not being challenged enough.

The best cure is an actual playmate, and most children drop the habit when they enter school, or when they have an active social life, except during periods of loneliness or occasional depression.

After the age of 5 or 6, the more socialized and interesting the child's life can become, the less the need for imaginary playmates.

LISPING

Lisping (the inability to properly make the "S" or related sounds — ch, j, sh, s, etc.) is not uncommon during the early speech development of the child, since it represents one of the most difficult sounds. It becomes a problem when it persists after the child has entered school age.

The causes may be organic, involving malformation of the teeth or the oral cavity, though this is rare. The most common causes include a child's desire for continuing an attention-getting habit of baby talk, emotional immaturity, or poor parental examples of speech. The practice often becomes a habit after the need has left, and usually produces emotional side-effects.

Bakwin suggests that, because of the emotional factors involved, the parents, themselves, should not attempt to correct the problem, but should refer the child to a speech therapist. The child's faulty speech can usually be attacked directly, with the emphasis on the gradual correction of the sound itself. When emotional immaturity is involved, a more mature role on the part of the child is desirable.

LYING

Children live in a world in which certain social or economic "lies," such as misrepresenting one's age, a missing price tag on an object, etc., are prevalent, and even encouraged by the parents. It is not always easy for the child to determine at an early age which modified or "white" lies are appropriate, and which are actually lies as such.

The causes of lying are as varied as the degree of the falsehoods, and include some of the following: to gain attention or status; revenge against a peer or adult; to make one's enemy look "bad"; to enhance a dull life with exaggerated episodes; to avoid humiliating consequences of one's behavior; and to avoid punishment, which is generally the greatest single cause of childhood lying.

Childhood lies prosper when they are repeatedly successful. The reinforcement of getting away with a lie tends to perseverate the practice.

The simplest and best prevention is to identify and eliminate the need for lying. The parents, themselves, must recognize that their pattern of social lying may be a contributing factor, and should be encouraged toward frankness in the presence of the child. The child should learn that although an act might bring undesirable consequences, immediate punishment never follows a truthful statement.

Children usually lie to escape immediate, rather than long-range consequences. The child's need for lying, as well as the easy opportunity for lying, must be avoided.

MASTURBATION

Infant masturbation during the first 2 years of life is not uncommon. The cause during the first few months is unknown; however, many physical causes after the early months have been considered. These include localized irritation from tight clothes, remaining in wet diapers, intestinal disorders such as worms, stroking the child's thighs, etc. The child's pleasurable habit of scratching or rubbing the affected area becomes enjoyable and is continued. Research suggests that frequently the infant does have an orgasm, although without an ejaculation. There is no evidence that this is physically or psychologically harmful to the infant. Infants tend to give up the habit at age 2 or 3 years unless it offers certain psychic rewards in terms of parental anxiety or concern. The unhappy or bored infant tends to continue somewhat longer.

The parents need to be reassured that this pleasurable infant habit is not abnormal, nor does it suggest future sex problems. Before age 6 months certain physical restraints or diversions may be useful (arrangement of the diapers so as to keep the legs farther apart, providing abundant rattles or toys in the crib, teaching him to sleep with his hands outside the blankets, control through medication, etc.). Scoldings by the parent should, of course, be avoided.

As the infant grows into childhood, the same causes may bring about a recurrence of the pleasurable sensation. As with infants, the parents need have no great concern, unless there is evidence that it is over-done. The problems connected with the "cure" are generally more harmful to the child than the act itself. The child's feelings of guilt or embarrassment can drive the child further underground for secrecy. The best management is through providing means by which the childhood masturbation is inconvenient. These include a full and active life, interests, hobbies, outdoor games, competitive games and sports, social contacts, selection of clothes which discourage easy access to the genitals, etc. The child should be physically tired when he goes to bed, and should never be sent to bed early as punishment or as convenience for the parents. In prolonged or excessive cases, medication can be useful.

The habit among adolescents is natural and unavoidable, and is far from incidental or accidental. It can become a problem through parental mismanagement. The adolescent should have sex presented to him by his parents as a natural aspect of human relationships, and he should see a happy marital adjustment in his parents. The problems are compounded when the parents are divorced or incompatible.

The adolescent needs successful social experiences with the opposite sex, and as in the case of the younger child, a full and active successful physical and social life. Much excessive masturbation is brought on by fantasies in which the unsuccessful adolescent can now see himself as a success.

Above all, the adolescent must not be lectured, scolded, or shamed. The habit needs treatment only when it is practiced to excess, or when it involves feelings of deep shame or guilt. The greater the adolescent's feelings of self-worth and the happier the parental material adjustment, the less are the chances for excessive maturbation on the part of the adolescent.

MOTHER-FIXATION (MOMISM)

The primary cause of this excessive emotional attachment of a son to his mother is the domination and smothering of the son by his mother, who though often competent in managing affairs, business, etc., is basically an insecure and demanding person. The father is usually absent or passive. Unless corrected, the condition becomes steadily worse, until the young man becomes so dominated and dependent that he never becomes totally freed, and if he marries, tends to marry a mother-image.

The referral for help rarely comes from the parents in these cases, but more often from the school regarding the boy's immature behavior and lack of individual responsibility. The mother must be made to see that her over-protection of the child is keeping him from developing emotionally. The father, if present, should be encouraged to take a more active role in his son's activities. Nursery school, church groups, scouting, YMCA, etc., or any social activity which gives the boy interests away from the mother's domination are to be encouraged.

MOTOR PATTERNING

In the past decade, the use of the theory of cerebral dominance to explain dyslexia or motor difficulties, and the technique of motor patterning (commonly known as the Doman-Delacate method) to remedy this difficulty have been alternately praised by parents and viewed with caution by professionals. The Doman-Delacate method, advanced by the Institutes for the Achievement of Human Potential in Philadelphia, is basically a sensorimotor approach designed to "program" the brain by means of prescribed sensorimotor exercises. The treatment is based on human development theory, and involves parent activity in working with the child.

Jastak and many others have been very critical of the method, feeling that the "element of truth" in the cerebral dominance theory has been exaggerated out of proportion as being a primary factor in reading disability, so that remedial reading is slighted. The lack of objective research is usually cited as a major criticism of the method.

The school psychologist is often expected to discuss this matter with parents or parent groups, and should be conversant with the arguments for and against the method. Actually, whenever considerable time is spent with a child on a one-to-one basis, such time is most often beneficial to the child, and such is most probably the case with this method. The dearth of actual research in the professional journals to show clear, scientific evidence of the success of the method, however, should serve as a caution. To the writer's knowledge, no such research has as yet appeared.

NAIL BITING

Nail biting is most commonly found among tense, nervous children and adults, and is frequently imitated by children whose parents are nail biters. Studies suggest that about one-half of the children are or have been nail biters, and that the incidence is much greater among boys than girls. The habit usually gradually declines after about age 12.

The practice is usually engaged in when the child feels a need for the relief of tension. The treatment, therefore, should be directed toward the source of the child's anxiety, rather than toward the habit. The parents or teachers should make certain that the child does not feel real or imagined pressures on his performance, and that the expectancies placed on the child are realistic.

PHOBIAS

A phobia is an unrealistic fear, which may be accompanied by a compulsive act, such as avoidance, running, etc., in certain situations. Phobias are generally the outcome of a traumatic experience with which the person associates feelings of guilt. Later, these feelings cause the person to repress the guilt to avoid the anxiety, thus bringing on the abnormal fear (phobia) in a new disguise.

Phobias are less common in children than in adolescents and adults. When they appear in a child, they are usually transient and innocuous, and are more often found among the more timid and fearful. Adequate social contacts and a free, frank discussion regarding the traumatic episode can usually ease the minor situations in children.

PREJUDICE

Prejudices may rise from one's normal preference for the familiar, coupled with the natural resistance to strange customs or persons, which add to one's insecurity. Its basis is generally in identification, and in young children is usually little more than an imitation of parents or peers.

Unfortunately, the elimination of prejudice involves a long process of retraining and reinforcement, and often meets resistance when it is handled too speedily or obviously.

The surest way to minimize or eliminate the problem is through building the person's feeling of security. The more secure the individual is, the more he can afford to look at the problem objectively. The older the child is, the more easily he can be made to see the relationship between prejudice and ignorance; the vanity of the junior high or high school pupil is often an open channel for intelligent, rational discussions.

PROFANITY

Almost every young child, especially a boy, will experiment with profanity at one time or another. It is usually his attempt to be "adult," to draw attention of adults, to get revenge on his parents, or to gain status with a peer.

Profanity must be treated in a calm, reasonable manner, and unlike tantrums or aggressive behavior, can be handled when the act occurs. The parent must not appear shocked, horrified, or amused, which is the reaction the child is seeking. Rather, the parent can simply explain that there are words which can and those which should not be used.

Though parents are prone to be quick to explain that their child did not hear the language at home, more often than not the child *did* hear it at home. The common practice of parental profanity for comic emphasis or for catharsis is seen as permissable by the child, or as a means of the child's arousing the parents with the parent's own weapon.

RETENTION IN A GRADE
(SEE ACCELERATION)

If there are pitfalls in the acceleration of a child to an advanced grade, these are compounded in the case of a child repeating a grade. No matter how the situation is disguised, the child often still sees himself as having failed. The research continues to suggest that children who repeat a grade do not necessarily do better work than had they gone ahead with their chronological age peers.

There are, however, many cases in which the retention seems advisable and in the best total interests of the child. The following factors should be considered:

1. *C.A.* The child whose birthdate falls in the last half of the calendar year (July through December 1st) would be in the younger half of the class, and less likely to be penalized by adding a semester or year to his academic life.

2. *IQ* The very superior child, (with an IQ of over 130) should not usually need to repeat a grade in order to catch up on his academic work, as he should be able to do his work with relative ease, with proper motivation and assistance. On the other hand, the slow learner will probably always achieve below his grade placement, and retention will not alleviate this discrepancy. In addition, research on school dropouts indicates that these pupils often leave school because of increased chronological age. It is probably the child in the middle ranges of intellectual ability who has the best chance of profiting from retention.

3. *Physical Size.* Though size is a relatively superficial factor among adults, this is not so among children. The early maturing child, already larger than his peers, might well suffer indignities if he found himself in a group of still smaller children.

4. *Present Grade Placement.* Retention should normally take place during the early years. Kindergarten, first, or second grade pupils feel far less stigma than those in the third grade or above.

5. *Sex.* Because of the rate of maturation, and the problems of physical size, the retention of a girl usually poses more problems than a boy, just as the acceleration of a boy poses more difficulties than a girl.

6. *Siblings.* If a child has a sibling in the grade for which he is being considered, family difficulties could arise.

7. *Peer Relationships.* Is the child a part of the community-neighborhood group with which he closely identifies? Would his placement in another grade affect his feelings as far as his peers are concerned?

8. *Parental Approval.* The parents should be in favor of the proposed move (some districts insist on parental approval). If the retention serves only to antagonize the parents, it may reflect itself in the entire family relationship and affect the child's attitude toward school. If the parents approve, the child's chances for success are, of course, enhanced.

9. *Child's Attitude.* Ideally, the pupil himself should take part in the decision. If he is a part of the planning and can see that this is a chance for him to catch up on things he missed, that he may now be one of the leaders instead of a follower, etc., he invariably has a more favorable attitude toward the move. Some teachers have used the technique of introducing a child at the beginning of the year who chose to repeat a grade in order to get a better foundation in some of the skills he felt he had missed. The teacher explains that the child wanted to make sure that he had mastered the material before he went on to another grade.

It is advisable for a school district to have a policy regarding retention, lest there be varying philosophies in each school within the district. Most surely, a child should never repeat a grade more than once. The best insurance is the early identification of the child for whom the move might be necessary. The pre-first grade has proved a successful device for avoiding the image of failure. The immature, disadvantaged, or slow child who appears likely to not succeed in the first grade goes, instead, into the pre-first grade, which is a blend of kindergarten and the first grade. Upon the completion of this grade, he goes directly into the first grade (or possibly the second).

RUNNING AWAY

The two main causes of running away are (1) a desire for excitement and adventure, and (2) a fantasy in which the child sees the parents as being sorry for the way in which they have treated the child, and in which they gladly welcome him home.

If adventure is the cause, the family might consider exciting home or club activities, hobbies, family projects, or outings which make the child's home life more interesting. If the cause is revenge or punishment of the parents, the family now needs to consider the reasons for the child's behavior. When the child first returns, the parental attitude is important. Criticism or corporal punishment only serve to increase the antagonism. The parents must be understanding, consider the child's complaints, and assure him that he is needed and appreciated at home. Nervous reactions by the parents may reinforce the child's episode and increase the chances for a recurrence, hence, the dialogue should be calm and relaxed.

SCHOOL PHOBIA

Every school psychologist at one time or another will be confronted with the difficult problem of school phobia, a child who resists or refuses to go to school. The child may be unaware of the causes of the anxiety, but may be tense, nauseous, tearful, or defiant. The child may even induce a fever, and may use any means available to stay at home, illness being the most logical. This disorder is generally found more often in girls than in boys, and is seldom found in those with dull-normal or retarded ability.

The original causes of the problem are believed to be related to a separation anxiety, based on, and too often encouraged by, a persisting emotional tie with the mother. The child later is not as reluctant to go to school as he is concerned about leaving or manipulating the mother. The condition then becomes triggered by a "legitimate" excuse or minor incident at school, such as a threatening teacher or peer, a brief illness from which the child does not wish to recover, etc. The father is often the passive parent in such cases. School phobia is most commonly tied in with the mother-child relationship.

As might be expected, the prognosis is poorer when the child is older. The child should return to school immediately. The longer he stays away, the more difficult the problem becomes. The child might stay in the nurse's office, the principal's office, anywhere at school rather than at home. Hopefully, the child eventually sees the classroom as more rewarding than a lonely office, since he is not permitted to stay where he wants — at home.

Meanwhile, the parent must be made to see that the child feels a dependence on the parent which should gradually give way to more self-initiated behavior on the part of the child. Traditionally, mothers in such cases have been prone to blame certain conditions in the school for the problem, and are reluctant to assume a share of the responsibility for the problem. Once the mother sees this, however, the prognosis becomes better. The more severe cases may have to be referred to a psychiatrist. In some cases, medical control has reduced the anxiety of the child, making the return to school somewhat easier.

SELF-INITIATED BEHAVIOR

There are several methods currently used which induce the child to assume responsibility for his own behavior, which is the most successful means by which a child can become motivated to do his school work or manage his behavior.

The teacher cannot continually *tell* a child to get to work, to study, to behave, etc., any more than he can continually advise appropriate punishment if the child does not behave.

1. *Systematic Exclusion.* One method of literally "forcing" responsibility for his own actions upon the child, himself, is through systematic exclusion, introduced by Dr. David Keirsey in the 1950's. This plan is most effective for the more severe or prolonged cases, but can be modified for the less severe offenders. The method, as the name implies, is highly systematized, and places the entire load or responsibility directly upon the child.

By a clearly understood contractual agreement (which may or may not use the actual contract) between the child and his teacher, an agreement is made in which the child is told that the school can no longer be responsible for telling him to do this or that, and that from now on, it is the child, himself, who must assume the responsibility. (The teacher will never *tell* the pupil to work, study, behave, or whatever the offense has been).

Optimally, a conference is held with the child, the teacher, the psychologist or counselor, the parents, and perhaps the principal. At this staging conference, as Dr. Keirsey calls it, the entire plan is laid out to the child. The ceremonial aspect of this staging conference is often as effective as the conference itself. The child is told that staying in school is a privilege, and that if he fails to live up to this contract for the specified time (by acts such as talking, "jabbing," not working, etc.) he instantly loses this privilege for the rest of the day. There is to be nothing punitive about the conference or about his being sent home,

nor should the teacher lecture the child in any way. The child, by a prearranged signal, is merely excused, goes to the principal's office, and then home.

The plan must have the complete cooperation of the school administration and the parents. The pattern will completely break down if one of the parties involved does not perform his role objectively and according to the rules. The parents may be sympathetic to the child's predicament at being home, but may not engage in any "I told you so's," or in any way rebuke the child for being sent home. Any punitive steps merely serve as a secondary reinforcement to the child, just as a spanking is often its own reward. The child must see the parents as interested, but *not* emotionally involved, merely as necessary objective parts of the total plan.

Often a teacher will say that he has tried this before, but that it does not work. The plan *will* work if it is followed to the letter and without exception. For example, the teacher must not say to the child, "Well, I'll overlook it this time, but the next time it happens, you must leave." The teacher, who has perhaps the most difficult role, *must* always, and without emotion, simply give the signal (a nod toward the door, etc.) the moment the offence occurs.

The child eventually sees himself as the *only* one responsible for his behavior. His parents cannot *make* him conform — his teacher cannot — *only he* can decide if he is to stay in school. If each adult performs his role according to the plan, the child sees going home as anything but a reward, and as a situation which he has created and could have avoided.

2. *Contingency Management.* Contingency management, devised by Dr. Laurence Peter (USC) and Dr. Marvin Daley (Utah State U.) has been successfully used in the special education classes at Visalia, Calif., under Dr. Harry Rosenberg, Director of Special Education. The basic premise of the plan is that behavior itself, rather than food or other rewards, becomes the reinforcer. The plan is really *reinforcement* techniques, rather than operant conditioning, in which another type of reinforcement is given.

Activities are selected according to whether they would be called "low probability behavior" (the less desirable activities on the part of the student, such as subject matter work, math, reading, etc.) or "high probability behavior" (recreational activities such as listening to records, puzzles, etc.).

The motivation for the child performing the low probability tasks is his privilege of performing the high probability tasks at the completion of the former. The classroom is designed to permit the child to move to the area of the high probability task when the other has been successfully completed, without disrupting the rest of the class. Thus, the room is divided into task and activity areas.

The students are taught to not rush to the activity area on completion of the work, but to go in an orderly manner when given permission by the teacher. The class members all begin the task at the same time, and ideally the entire class should finish within a few minutes of each other, so that for the most part, the class is together in either the task area or the reinforcement area. Usually, the student who has been delaying the completion of his work becomes motivated to finish when he sees the others gradually leaving for the reinforcement area.

Consistency on the part of the teacher is naturally the focal point in the success of the plan. It has been highly successful in motivating younger EMR and EH children to work diligently and orderly. The work periods must be short, and the reinforcement period should probably last from 5 to 8 minutes. Activities not finished during one task period may be carried over into the next thus the tasks must be carefully planned as to expected length. The teacher needs to provide enough work for about 15 minutes. The activities vary according to the level of the children.

This plan is amazingly simple, yet has been so easy to initiate and so profitable to the pupils that it deserves careful consideration for use as a means of motivating children to work without urging from the teacher.

3. *Behavior Modification (Operant Conditioning)*. This pattern is so widely known and used, especially with EMR and EH classes, that it needs no detailed description in this section. Behavior modification, or operant conditioning, is a means of teaching and reinforcing certain desired behavior in children. The theory behind behavior modification is simply that a child will tend to repeat that type of behavior which is reinforced, and to eventually reject that behavior which is *not* reinforced. Eventually the desired behavior becomes its own reinforcement and becomes habitual (operant). One must wait for the desired behavior to take place before reinforcement is given, rather than promise the reward if and when the behavior does occur.

Some practical questions must be asked by the teacher: Exactly what behavior am I trying to modify or produce? Is it possible for the child to learn this behavior? Is the demand I am making reasonable?

Then, the teacher reinforces the child's behavior by a simple reward (a pat on the shoulder, bits of candy, etc.). The reinforcement should come as soon as possible after the behavior. Once established, the positive reinforcement should be spaced so that it need not be given every time the act occurs. Consistency on the part of the teacher becomes the key factor in such forms of conditioning behavior.

Behavior modification and its implication to the schools is discussed in great length in Woody's new book, *Behavioral Problem Children in the Schools*.

SHYNESS

Shyness is not as pathological as many fear. Follow-up studies of shy children referred to clinics have shown that the shy children, though tending to continue to be shy as adults, did not necessarily manifest adult symptoms of maladjustment. They tended to select occupations or professions which offered shelter or security and to marry more outgoing partners. The marriages were as successful as with the average population. In short, the shy child who is given an opportunity to develop in his own way tends to have a satisfactory adult adjustment.

Opportunities, however, can be provided the child to succeed in secure situations. He should not be pushed into overwhelming situations to force him out of his shyness.

Discussing shyness with a child usually tends to only worsen the situation.

SIBLING RIVALRY

Jealousy or rivalry among children of a family is a normal thing. Though it is unpleasant and undesirable, its appearance is usually inevitable and often superficial, being nurtured by the parents' overreaction to verbalisms or actions by the jealous child.

Jealousy is usually more pronounced in the first-born, although it is also found in varying degrees in the other children, and even in large families, when the children learn they must divide the mother's attention. The first-born child tends to resent the protection he sees given the younger siblings.

The pattern usually worsens if the younger sibling is born during the older child's pre-school years, when the latter is not yet in school and is not yet able to handle the problem he sees. When the older child is in school at the birth of the younger, the problem generally tends to be less severe. It is usually more severe when the siblings are of the same sex, and is usually more common among girls than boys. The manifestations are usually hostility, an attempt to return to infantile patterns, demands for attention, self-punishment, bed-wetting, refusing to eat without being fed, etc.

It may also be compounded by immaturity on the part of the parent, such as demanding, insecure mothers who compete with the children for attention or favors, or by fathers who set rigid standards for obedience or comparisons.

A few do's and don'ts are given as preliminary steps in attempting to alleviate the problem:

1. *Avoid comparisons.* Do not compare one child with another, even by implication.

2. The parents must make certain they *are* being fair to all the children. Perhaps the jealous child is correct in believing that one sibling is getting a disproportionate amount of attention.

3. The parent should allow for a private time for each child. Even if the time is only 5 minutes or less, each child needs to know that a certain period of uninterrupted time is his own. Sometimes it is desirable to keep the older child up at night a few minutes longer, letting this be his private time. The satisfaction is even greater to the older child, since staying up later is seen as a special favor in our culture.

4. No child outgrows the need to be told by his parents that he is loved. All children need this feeling of comfort and reassurance.

SOCIAL ISOLATION

Various sociometric techniques have been devised by which the teacher can make a periodical assessment of the group social climate within the classroom. Without such techniques, it is easy for the teacher to overrate the academically proficient or well-mannered pupil socially, and to tend to underrate a child socially who may not be academically adequate or who may not appear to the teacher to have desirable social qualities. Sociometric techniques have their limitations, and it must be recognized that they present only one clue in the child's social picture; however, they can be most helpful in focusing attention on the group structure in a class toward enhancing intergroup relations, re-seating pupils, assigning work-study groups, or identifying and assisting rejected or isolated pupils.

In presenting a sociogram to the class, the pupils are simply asked to list their first, second, and third choices of a companion for seating, work projects, field trips, etc. The responses are then tabulated by applying scores of 3 for a first choice, 2 for second, and 1 for third choice (and a minus 1 for those pupils who were listed as one whom the student would rather *not* be with).

A large circle is drawn on a piece of paper, with each child included within the circle. The boys names are usually put within a small triangle and the girls names in a small circle, with connecting lines between the two or more which were mutually chosen. The child's composite score can also be written within his triangle or circle, so that the teacher can identify at a glance the social cliques, rejections, isolates, etc.

Every attempt must then be made to seat the child in the manner he requested, to keep the technique "honest," although it now becomes possible to include the rejected or isolated child in a group of his choosing without hurting the social climate of the group or cluster.

STEALING

Stealing is engaged in at one time or another by virtually every child, and has one or more causes: the child's actual need or desire to acquire or to hoard; a desire for objects or money of which he feels he has been deprived; he may steal to give away, in order to demonstrate his generosity or bravery to his peers; for revenge against adults or peers.

The child's reputation and integrity are vital. The child must not be called or considered a thief. Many parents become defensive and exaggerate the importance of the act, applying adult connotations to what is a normal childhood activity, and try to shame the child in an effort to show their displeasure. The crime is rarely as damaging as the cure.

Some parents have adopted the practice of keeping loose change in family "secret places," such as a jar in the cupboard. The child is made aware of the presence of the money, and is told that this is for minor "emergencies," such as the paper boy's collection, the ice-cream wagon, etc. The child is told he may use the money when he considers it necessary, but that he should remember or make note of the amount, which *may* later be deducted from the child's allowance with the child's knowledge. The child's ready access to the money, combined with the feelings of trust and his own personal responsibility, tend to reduce the need for stealing.

Parents should examine their domination of the child. Does he have an adequate allowance? Does he have opportunities to make his own decisions and assume responsibility? The child may be stealing to get revenge for unfair treatment, or may be expressing his need to be a part of the family planning, needs, sharing, etc.

STUTTERING*

Most school districts have a trained speech therapist on the staff who is prepared and qualified to provide therapy to stutterers. If, however, the school psychologist must provide the therapy, there are a few points to consider. The young stutterer does not always have a desire for therapy for one or more of several reasons:

1. Thinking or talking about stuttering may temporarily make it worse, or make it seem worse.

2. He is confused about what is wrong with him.

3. Since other people have not talked about it, perhaps he feels he had better not, either. It may be unmentionable, unspeakable.

4. The whole experience may possibly be laden with shame, guilt, fear, and frustration.

5. He does not know *how* to talk about it.

6. Talking, itself, has become hard for him.

7. Avoidance of everything connected with the problem has become inviting, while confrontation, at the beginning at least, is much harder.

Based on this, the psychologist might consider several issues:

Motivating the child toward therapy. Recognizing that therapy is generally *not* the child's idea, continued lack of motivation suggests a need to postpone the therapy, pending the development of a more friendly family or school climate, or a greater readiness for change on the part of the child. However, a child can often be motivated if a friendly, honest dialogue can be established. Is the child concerned about his speech? Does he *want* to change it? Ask him if he would like to speak more easily — even stutter more easily. Pick out a particular word that bothers him (usually his name), and show him that he can change what he does on this word. Reward his efforts, and always try to build up his curiosity about what people call stuttering. Help him want to explore the mystery — because he is interested. Has he ever really heard himself stuttering? Help him become curious to listen on a tape, to watch himself in a mirror. Remind him he can go on talking in his familiar ways, or he can learn easier ways of talking.

Subgoals of the Therapy. Other subgoals might develop as the child's language and feelings develop. The frank approach about trying to help the problem is currently generally considered more relevant

than the former "fun and games" method of attacking the issue, although it may sometimes be more appropriate to use the latter in the case of the very young (below age 7 or if very immature). If the child is embarrassed or the stuttering is most severe, the therapist can merely keep talking — about his work, his successes with others, how he knows how they feel, his particular interest in stuttering, etc.

Help the child realize that stuttering is something he *does* rather than something that happens *to* him. Some have used the technique of having the child speak until he finds a word he cannot say, then both can explore new ways of producing the word or sound, e.g., from the "P" in Paul to potato, with the accent on the second syllable.

Some therapists stutter with the child, stuttering in unison with him, but providing a model for better speech and better stuttering. Children rarely stutter in choral speaking.

Regarding Escaping. Convince the child that his attempts to escape from stuttering make the stuttering worse. He needs to lose his fear of stuttering and to stop avoiding the feared words and situations. In this sense, group therapy is often better, so that one who has learned to tackle the feared words can serve as a model.

Use any situational means of building the child's self-confidence and esteem. This is most easily done by providing the child opportunities for doing the things he already does well, and by his gradually learning other things which bring him reward.

Facial Grimaces. Help the stutterer rid himself of facial contortions, jaw jerks, etc., by showing him that he can stutter just as well without them. Have him practice stuttering without facial movements.

Stuck on Sounds. Show him that when he is stuck (blocked on a sound he is unable to produce), that struggling and growing panicky only intensify the problem. Approach the feared words in a normal fashion. The child must learn not to prepare for the feared words, but to discover that he can say words similar to those words without the facial and emotional preparation. Reassure the stutterer that the fear of stuttering is not always followed by stuttering. In groups, have the speaking pupil hold up his hand when he thinks he is going to stutter on a word, then show him how seldom he actually does.

Regarding Regression. Be prepared for the fact that the stutterer may temporarily grow worse. This may be due to several things: a reflection of real

*Acknowledgment: "Treatment of Young Stutterers in the School," 4th printing, Speech Foundation of America, 1968, Pub. #4.

progress, hidden stuttering due to previous evasion of words now coming into the open; the child may be speaking more, or he may be testing the examiner. Remember that temporary regression is far better than a static condition.

Regarding the Child's Teacher. Enlist the teacher's aid by reminding him that this must be a team effort. Inquire about the child's progress, or lack of it, in the class. Find out under what conditions the child is most likely to stutter.

TEMPER TANTRUMS

Except for the early primary grades, tantrums are usually a problem of the home more than the school. The causes are varied, but may include the following:

1. Inconsistent methods of control by an adult.

2. The child may have found that the tantrum is a profitable means of getting his own way.

3. Conflicting standards between parent, home, and school, parent and grandparent, etc.

4. Prolonged periods of illness, especially during the pre-school years, during which the child received a disproportionate amount of attention and became used to getting his own way.

5. Overcritical, nagging, or over-solicitous parents.

6. Imitation by the child of observed adult outbursts.

The treatment must result in a re-learning by the child. He must learn that a tantrum *never* results in a victory. The first step is to determine which of the above causes may have contributed to the condition, and to remove them. Never talk to or reason with the child during the outburst. The reasoning, if any, should be done some time after the tantrum is over, and little reference should be made directly to it. The tantrum itself should not bring attention; rather, praise or reinforcement should be given for the desirable behavior when *it* happens. The parents, themselves, must provide the example of calm, considerate behavior.

When it is actually necessary to remove the child during a tantrum because of danger to other children, upset to a class, etc., it should be done without lectures or revenge, but calmly and without comment. A tantrum quickly subsides without an audience.

THUMB-SUCKING

Thumb-sucking is usually established during the early months of life, especially during sleep. It normally gradually ceases during the second year, but may persist another year or so. The undesirable effects of thumb-sucking have been greatly exaggerated. Aside from minor irritations to the thumb and dentition, the habit is not known to be harmful. It becomes psychologically undesirable when it continues after the age of 5 or 6, but even at that age it is usually practiced only at bedtime.

The parents should be apprised as to the relative harmlessness of the habit, as opposed to the possible harm of corrective means. Restraints are generally more harmful than the habit, which is brought on by fatigue, stress, restlessness, or boredom. When the child is at an age of reason (5 or 6), the parent can usually appeal in a quiet manner to the child's desire to terminate the habit. If the habit persists after age 7, the parents might consult an orthodontist.

TICS

Tics largely involve the face and neck, although they may affect most parts of the body. The old fear that a tic was in some way related to masturbation has largely been discarded. The greatest incidence is in the childhood years, and usually disappears during adolescence.

Minor tics come and go, especially among boys, when minor unresolved conflicts confront the child. Family tensions are a major cause of persistent childhood tics, although even then they are generally not as pathological as they are annoying. Parents should ignore the tic, but investigate the possible sources of irritation.

Severe or persisting tics suggest a medical evaluation. In some cases, medication (Benardryl) has been rcommended. Often, when the tic has disappeared through medical help, it does not recur.

TRUANCY

Truancy has multiple possible causes; by far the most common is parental attitude and lack of supervision. Families in which both parents work, are difficult to reach by phone, or are indifferent to the problem (which is most generally the case), make it easy and inviting for the child to become truant. Other causes include: a delayed recovery from illness, in which the child spends much more time at home "recuperating" from a simple illness such as a cold; peer relationships at school; truant friends who serve as an incentive to stay away; becoming far behind in academic work; a mild form of running away from home; mild retardation, in which case the work may be too difficult; intellectual superiority, in which case the work is too easy. School truancy is a more aggressive and less pathological form of school phobia.

In almost every case, the correction lies first in exploring the home situation, in which the problem is generally rooted. The solution lies in locating and identifying the specific cause, which is usually easily remedied.

UNDERACHIEVEMENT

The underachieving pupil is one of the most common yet complex problems confronting the school psychologist, and is surely the basis for more referrals by teachers than any other issue.

"Underachievement" simply means performance markedly below one's evidenced potential. Achievement is a symptom rather than an entity.

The first step in the remediation is, of course, to determine the pupil's potential. The pupil with a lower mental age than his peers may be achieving below grade level but *not* underachieving. If an elementary pupil obtains an average score on the WISC or Binet, yet is achieving academically a year or more below his class level, the psychologist may consider one or a combination of several alternatives.

Try to identify the area of underachievement. Is it in specific areas, as revealed by group achievement tests or the WRAT? Find if there is a discrepancy between the reading and arithmetic scores, for example, or between reading and spelling. If the difficulty is in a specific area such as reading, rather than general underachievement, the task becomes one of further breaking down the disability. Is it in speed, accuracy, comprehension, as determined by the group tests or in individual reading tests such as the Gilmore Oral Reading Test? The WRAT ('65 edition) has an excellent section of specific individual remediation for underachievement. This handbook also contains specific suggestions for remediation of specific areas.

General underachievement is a far different matter, and usually involves a much more complex analysis. Unfortunately, underachievement is not often remedied at school. Though the problem may stem from the pupil's low self-concept and from his fear of failure at school, it is more often than not a product of parental domination. In either case, the underachieving pupil usually sees himself as inadequate. No pupil wants to be an underachiever, but would rather say to himself that he *will not* rather than that he *cannot* achieve.

The problem becomes one of gradually making the child responsible for his own actions. One cannot teach a child to work. One can neither lecture nor advise the underachiever.

For a change to take place in school achievement, the pupil must feel free to perceive himself as the only one who can make decisions for himself, and as being able to make the right decision. He must know that no one can make decisions for him. Most underachievers have a history of overprotection, of having decisions made *for* them. This is usually initiated by the parents and sometimes reinforced by the teacher.

The school cannot give responsibility to the pupil, or *tell* him to work, but *can* create situations in which the student feels that the steps are minute, and that the chances for success are great. The school must not expect long assignments from one who has done virtually nothing, but must realize that short, easy assignments, successfully completed, are the forerunner for these. Only as the underachiever sees success can he build toward self-initiated behavior. This feeling of personal responsibility for one's own action is perhaps the only true direction to take with the chronic underachiever.

References

Attwell, A., "A Suggestion For Teaching the Underachiever," *Cal. Math, Council Bull.*, 22, 1965.

Attwell, A., and Clabby, D., *The Retarded Child: Answers to Questions Parents Ask*, Los Angeles, Cal. Western Psychological Services, 1971.

Attwell, A., "Underachievement in School: A Suggested Remedy," *Elem. School Couns. and Guid. J.*, Dec., 1968.

Bakwin, H., and Bakwin, R., *Clinical Management of Behavior Disorders in Children*, W. B. Saunders Co., Philadelphia, 1968.

Boder, Elena, "Dyslexia . . . ," in *Learning Disabilities*, Vol 2, H. Myklebust, ed., New York, Grune & Stratton, In press.

Delacato, C. H., *Diagnosis and Treatment of Speech and Reading Problems*, Springfield, Ill., Chas Thomas Co., 1964.

Hewett, Frank, *The Emotionally Disturbed Child In the Classroom*, Allyn and Bacon, 1970.

Jastak, J. F. and Jastak, S. R., *WRAT Manual*, Wilmington, Del., Guidance Assoc. Inc., 1965.

Money, J., *Reading Disability*, Johns Hopkins Press, Baltimore, 1962.

Orton, J. L., The Orton Story, *Bulletin of the Orton Society*, 7: 5-8.

Senn, M. J. and Solnit, A. J., *Problems in Child Behavior and Development*, Lea and Febeger, Philadelphia, 1968.

Verville, E., *Behavior Problems of Children*, W. B. Saunders Co., Philadelphia, 1968.

Woody, R., *Behavioral Problem Children in the Schools*, Appleton-Century-Croft, New York, 1969.

6. The School Psychologist and Special Education

The history of school psychology is closely tied to special education programs, for it was through this medium that many school districts first employed psychologists. Indeed, many psychologists are employed today because of special education. Since the first permissive (and later mandatory) programs, special education has undergone almost unbelievable growth.

Keeping abreast of the criteria for eligibility, admission, dismissal, transfer, etc., of pupils in these classes is virtually impossible, because of the frequent changes in legislation. Further, these criteria vary from state to state. Even the terminology is different.

The various sections of this chapter, therefore, have been written with regard to the current California legislation regarding special education classes, recognizing that future changes will be inevitable. The reader will find that the special education provisions in the various states will vary somewhat, and will need to consult the local State Education Code for the specific provisions.

Programs for the Mentally Retarded

Educable Mentally Retarded (EMR)

Among the pioneer programs in the field of special education are those for the mildly retarded (EMR). Established for the purpose of providing education at a slower, more individualized rate, the EMR classes now represent the largest single category of special education programs nationally.

The educable mentally retarded child, usually normal in appearance and behavior, has a special need to find acceptance at school and in the community. Economic self-sufficiency is also a goal of the program.

Children assigned to these classes are those who cannot profit from full-time instruction in regular classes, but who are able to learn academic subjects to the extent that they can maintain themselves as self-supporting adults.

Definition. A minor who, because of retarded intellectual development, is incapable of being educated efficiently and profitably through ordinary classroom instruction. (There is growing concern regarding the disproportionate number of minority children placed in programs for the retarded. The following expanded provisions have been developed to ensure that each child receives a complete and individual evaluation.)*

Screening. Group tests results may be used only for initial screening and referral, but should not be used as a basis for determining mental retardation. The following types of pupils should be routinely referred to the school psychologist and the local admissions committee for study:

1. Pupils more than 2 years behind normal grade placement with reference to their chronological age.
2. Pupils who are 2 or more years behind in academic achievement and who have been receiving near failing marks in the basic academic subjects. Referral for psychological services should be made before the minor's problems become severe.
3. Pupils who have failed basic skill subjects for 2 or more consecutive years.
4. Pupils falling below the 5th percentile on standardized achievement tests.
5. Pupils falling into the range of the mildly retarded on group mental ability tests.

Following is a list of group intelligence tests which can be used for screening and referral:

1. California Test of Mental Maturity, 1963 revision.
2. The Chicago Non-Verbal Examination.
3. The Culture-Fair Intelligence Test.
4. Henmon-Nelson Tests of Mental Ability — Revised Education.
5. Kuhlman-Anderson Intelligence Tests — 7th Edition.
6. Lorge Thorndike Intelligence Tests.
7. Otis-Lennon Mental Ability Tests.
8. Pintner General Ability Tests.
9. SRA (Primary Mental Abilities).
10. SRA (Tests of Educational Ability).
11. SRA (Tests of General Ability).

Each school district charged with the responsibility of establishing and maintaining special education programs for the mentally retarded should maintain an active screening and referral process. Referrals for

---

*Based upon Sept., 1969 Policy and Procedure bulletin sent to Calif. County and District Supts., by Joseph Rice, Bur. for Mentally Exceptional Children.

additional screening and possible individual evaluation might be made by:

1. The minor's parent and/or guardian.

2. Any teacher having instructional responsibilities for the minor.

3. A principal, vice-principal, counselor, school nurse, or social worker.

4. Other persons designated by the administrator for such responsibilities.

Individual Case Study. Certification of eligibility for placement requires careful analysis of the following information.

1. *Educational History*
   a. Specific statements from the minor's teacher regarding the strengths and weaknesses of the minor as demonstrated by observed behavior.
   b. Records of academic achievement including scores on group standardized tests.
   c. Teachers' reports on academic achievement in the classroom.
   d. Teachers' reports on observations of success and failure and the situation in which these occurred. This report should include the effect of success and failure on classroom behavior and pupil achievement as observed by the teacher.

2. *Psychological Evaluation*
   a. The psychological evaluation should include sufficient psychological tests to establish a valid estimate of intellectual functioning of the minor under consideration. One or more of the following approved individual intelligence tests must be administered:
      (1) Leiter International Performance Scale.
      (2) Stanford Binet (L-M).
      (3) Wechsler Adult Intelligence Scale (WAIS).
      (4) Wechsler Intelligence Scale for Children (WISC).
      (5) Wechsler Pre-School and Primary Scale of Intelligence (WPPSI).
      (6) Authorized Spanish versions of the Wechsler tests should be used as appropriate.
   b. One or more of the following supplemental tests may be used:
      (1) Arthur Point Scale of Performance Tests, Revised Form II.
      (2) Cattell Infant Intelligence Scale.
      (3) Columbia Mental Maturity Scale — Revised Edition.
      (4) Draw-A-Person (Goodenough)
      (5) Gesell Developmental Schedules.
      (6) Goodenough-Harris Drawing Test.
      (7) Full Range Picture Vocabulary.
      (8) Merrill-Palmer Pre-School Performance.
      (9) Peabody Picture Vocabulary Test.
      (10) Van Alstyne Picture Vocabulary.
   c. The program expectancies and academic standards being placed on the minor at the present time must be identified and evaluated.
   d. Evidence of prior experience or achievement on group and individual tests.
   e. Children coming from homes in which the primary spoken language is other than English should be interviewed and examined both in English and in the primary language. The examiner should make the assessment on the basis of the language most familiar to the child, and should utilize more than one instrument, including performance tests.
   f. If needed, the school psychologist should select an interpreter from the following, in order of preference:
      (1) A psychologist-trainee or intern enrolled in a professional training program, or a school psychologist competent in both languages.
      (2) Certificated employees of the district competent in both languages.
      (3) Classified employees of the district competent in both languages.
      (4) Recognized persons from the business and professional communities competent in both languages. Written parental approval should be obtained when non-credentialed persons serve as interpreters. The interpreter should then be instructed that he is to interpret, rather than to evaluate. The interpreter's name becomes part of the testing record.

Pupils returning to regular class from an EMR program should be placed with children of comparable age (based on the developmental, social, physical, and educational needs of the pupil), utilizing the persons most familiar with the pupil's needs.

In placing a child in an EMR class, *both* the verbal and performance sections must fall within the accepted range. For example, a child obtaining a qualifying score in the verbal and in the Full Scale of the WISC should *not* be placed if his performance score is above the qualifying range.

3. *Social, Economic, and Cultural Background*
   a. Information on the family background should be gathered. This information should be obtained through conferences with the parents and/or guardians, using the language which is fully understandable to the parents (guardians). This information should include:
      (1) Language used in the home.
      (2) Family mobility.
      (3) Occupational history and status of the parents.
      (4) Sibling relationships.
   b. Evidence of deprivation:
      (1) Isolation of home, family, and child within the environment.
      (2) Developmental materials within the home, such as educational toys, books, reading materials, etc.
      (3) Observations of the home environment reflecting factors which could influence the educational process.

Developmental History. A developmental history of each minor should be gathered during conferences with the parents. To establish mental retardation, the developmental records should reveal significant delays and/or retarded development in such behavior as walking, talking, appropriate affective responses, assumption of responsibility, obedience within the family structure, play activities, and peer relationships within the home and in the community.

Peer Relationships. A study of the minor's peer, classroom, and home relationships to determine if there are such inadequacies as:
a. Inability to maintain social roles.
b. Lack of friendship with age peers.
c. Inability to comprehend and respond to ordinary school and social demands.
d. Lack of lasting social involvement in the school and the home.

Health History. A report on the health and physical condition of the minor should include the results of any recent physical examinations and visual or auditory tests administered by the district. Any impairment in sensory or motor functioning should be noted, together with recommendations for educational and physical rehabilitation.

Miscellaneous. Other pertinent information that would contribute to the recommendations by the Admissions Committee.

Local Admissions Committee. In California, for example, the Local Admissions Committee consists of the following:

1. The pupil's teacher.

2. A school nurse or social worker.

3. The school psychologist who has individually examined the minor.

4. A school principal, supervisor, or designated administrator.

5. A school physician.

6. Other persons as the head of the school district may deem appropriate.

The following functions are performed by the Local Admissions Committee.

1. Careful consideration and complete analysis of the complete case study of each minor being recommended for placement in an EMR class (or a trainable mentally retarded, TMR, class).

2. Recommendations for appropriate educational placement are made after a full review of all the information available on the minor has been made. Specific efforts must be made by the committee to identify the best possible educational placement for the minor available within the district. Final recommendations of the committee include one of the following:
   a. Ineligible for placement in special education classes for the retarded; remain in regular class.
   b. Referral for consideration for other special education programs; meanwhile, remain in regular instructional program.
   c. Placement in special education programs for the mentally retarded for either special day class or an integrated program of instruction or into a TMR program.
   d. Trial placement in special education program with a specific period of time established for reconsideration.
   e. Request for additional study and psychological evaluation on which to base a recommendation.
   f. Other professional recommendations as indicated by individual cases.

3. Assignment to the appropriate program is recommended by a majority of the Admissions Committee, the school psychologist concurring. Where unanimous agreement is lacking, assignment is recommended on a trial basis, with a date established for reevaluation of the minor's progress.

4. A written report of the conference meeting of the Admissions Committee is prepared which includes the following:
   a. The committee's finding regarding the type and extent of the pupil's handicap and the relationship of this handicap to the educational needs of the pupil.
   b. The committee's findings regarding the ability of the pupil to profit from either of the programs (EMR, TMR) for the retarded, and any specific recommendations regarding particular methods of service from which the minor might be reasonably expected to profit.
   c. The committee's decision regarding eligibility and recommendations with respect to placement of the pupil in the most appropriate special education program.
   d. The names and titles of the committee members present at the meeting at which the recommendations were made.
5. Any members of the Admissions Committee dissenting from the final committee recommendation should attach to the final recommendations a statement of the reasons for the objection.

Conference with Parent. A conference is now held with the parent and/or guardian of the minor being considered, the conference being conducted by a member of the Admissions Committee. A discussion is held regarding the findings of the committee recommending special class placement, and the total program is discussed with the parent. Each conference is conducted in a language understandable to the parent, and, if necessary, an interpreter is provided to make sure the parent understands the special education placement. Every effort should be made to secure parental approval for the placement. (Parental approval is now mandatory in Calif.)

The parent, when feasible, should have the opportunity of visiting the special class to which the minor was recommended for placement. A report on this conference with the parent is made a part of the case study files of the minor.

Placement. It is recommended that the school undertake a transitional program to help the minor make the transition from regular class to the special education class. The benefits of the assignment should be explained to the pupil and the parent, and an opportunity to meet the special class teacher and to visit the class should be arranged. If indicated, the pupil might attend the special program only a part of the first few days.

Before attempting to work with the pupil, the special class teacher should be provided with a complete summary of the case study together with all the specific recommendations of the Admissions Committee. The school psychologist should provide the special class teacher with information concerning the pupil that will assist in developing appropriate learning activities for the minor. If the committee finds that a trial placement is indicated, a specific date should be set for reconsideration of the case and all persons participating in the minor's special education program should be alerted to this plan. Records of progress and adjustment should be kept during the trial placement. At the end of the trial placement, the pupil's case should be placed on the Admissions Committee's agenda for reevaluation.

Annual Review. An annual review of each minor placed in programs for the mentally retarded should be held by certain members of the Admissions Committee (the pupil's teacher, administrator, and the school psychologists are generally required), and continuance in the program is based on the findings of this group. This annual review consists of a study of data prepared and submitted from the following sources:

1. The pupil's special class teacher, including:
   a. General adjustment of the pupil to the school situation.
   b. Scholastic achievement, based on the ability on the minor. If possible, the academic level of achievement should be reflected.
   c. Brief summary of the minor's progress.
   d. Brief summary of the conference held with the minor's parents (guardians).
2. Reports from other instructional staff members regarding the performance of the minor.
3. Reports from other professional staff members involved in the educational program of the minor that would relate to changes in the minor's physical, social, or psychological condition. Where doubt exists as to the appropriateness of the placement, the Admissions Committee may request a complete reevaluation.

Complete Reevaluation (Every 3 Years). A complete reevaluation of each minor placed in special education classes for the mentally retarded should be made at least every 3 years. In addition, a complete reevaluation is made available at any time the Admissions Committee, the special class teacher, or other staff members involved in the program for the minor feel that this process is indicated due to a change in behavioral patterns. The person(s) requesting the reevaluation should set forth the reasons for such request on forms provided by the district for this purpose.

The complete reevaluation should be a joint endeavor of the Admissions Committee and other staff involved in the educational program of the minor concerned. The results of the reevaluation process should indicate one of the following:

1. Recommendation for continuation in the special education program

2. Suggestions for needed additional services and/or program adjustments

3. Withdrawal from the special education program and return to the regular instructional program

4. Transfer to another special education program

5. A recommendation to the administrative head of the district that the minor be withdrawn from the school program. This should be done only after complete and careful evaluation and exploring all available alternatives.

Transfer to Regular Instructional Program. A minor should be transferred from the special education program for the mentally retarded when the Admissions Committee finds that his needs can best be met in the regular instructional program. In arriving at this decision, the committee gives special consideration to the readiness of the pupil for placement in the less sheltered environment of a regular class, especially when he has been enrolled in the special education program for a number of years. The procedure of withdrawing a pupil from a special class is similar to that of assigning him to a special class. A reassignment procedure should be planned and implemented by the Admissions Committee, and it should include steps that guarantee to the minor a smooth transition.

Class Size. The maximum number of pupils generally allowed in an EMR class is 18. In a class in which the chronological age spread is greater than 4 years, the maximum enrollment should be 15. The minimum age in California, for admission to the program is 5 years 9 months (as of September 1st). The maximum age for admission to or retention in the elementary program is 14 years 9 months (as of September 1st). Exceptions to the latter may be made on recommendations of the Admissions Committee. Waiting lists are established when class enrollment limits are reached. When a vacancy occurs, a child is taken from the waiting list in the order in which placement has been recommended by the Admissions Committee. Decisions of the committee should be considered final.

Age Limits

1. *Mandated Programs*: All pupils of compulsory school age (6 through 18 years).

2. *Permissive Programs*: 5 years 9 months, and above compulsory school age (18 years), but less than 21 years. A pupil enrolled during the school year in which he becomes 21 may finish the school year.

Trainable Mentally Retarded (TMR)

For the past two decades, programs for the moderately retarded (TMR) have developed considerably on a national basis. With the gradual decentralization of the large state hospitals for the retarded, and the absorption of these youngsters into the community facilities, the natural result has been an increase in the number of programs for the moderately retarded.

Some of these pupils can become at least partially self-supporting, more cannot. Many will graduate to a sheltered workshop setting, where they can be gainfully employed and can contribute to their income and to society. All can and should learn at school that they have dignity and worth, and that they are making progress toward the goals of the program.

The test IQ's of these children are typically between 35 and 50. The program emphasizes communication and language development, self-help skills, and social awareness.

Definition. Those mentally retarded minors who are unable to profit from placement in classes for the educable mentally retarded, but who may be expected to benefit from special education facilities designed to educate and train them to further their individual acceptance, social adjustment, and economic usefulness in their homes and within a sheltered environment.

Eligibility. In California, pupils who are at least 4 years 9 months of age (as of September 1st), and who have not yet reached their eighteenth birthday may be considered. (Current legislation in many states is proposing a downward extension of the age limits). If a workshop placement is available and the pupil is considered eligible for such training, he may attend school one-half day, in connection with one-half day in the workshop between the ages of 18 and 21, if a workshop is available.

An IQ range of 35 through 50 is expected, though a leverage at either end is usually permitted. Eligibility of minors with IQ scores below 30 and above 55 should require special Admissions Committee recommendations. Further, eligibility for admission to TMR classes is dependent on the minor's ability to:

1. Be able to hear connected spoken language.

2. Be ambulatory to the extent that no undue risk to himself or others is involved in his daily work and play activities.

3. Be trained in toilet habits so that he has control over his body functions to the extent that it is feasible to keep him in school.

4. Be able to communicate to the extent that he is able to make his wants known and to understand simple directions.

5. Be developed socially to the extent that his behavior does not endanger himself and the physical well-being of other members of the group.

6. Be emotionally stable to the extent that group stimulation will not intensify his problems unduly.

7. Be ineligible for admission to special classes for the educable mentally retarded.

Screening, Individual Case Study, Local Admissions Committee, Parent Conference, Placement, Annual Review and Complete Reevaluations. (See section on educable mentally retarded).

Class Size. The maximum number of pupils is generally 12 per class. In addition to the teacher, a teacher aide for each class is recommended.

Goals. These pupils have the same needs shared by all children for developing their full potentials as individuals. The broad goals of the program, with specific task goals, are:

1. Developing as an individual.
   a. Strengthening self-awareness and positive self-concepts.
   b. Achieving greater independence through self-help.
   c. Using music and art to enhance personal development.
2. Growing within the environment.
   a. Learning to participate in a variety of situations.
   b. Developing suitable behavior in the home, the school, and the community.
   c. Strengthening the ability to communicate.
   d. Developing homemaking and vocational abilities.

Age Limits

1. *Mandated Programs.* All pupils age 6 through 18 (as of September 1st).
2. *Permissive Programs.* Ages 5 through 18. A pupil should stay in the program until the end of the school year in which he turns 21, if enrolled in the sheltered workshop.

Appropriate Psychological Tests. (The type of tests is not mandated as with the EMR).

1. Stanford-Binet, L.M.
2. Wechsler Scales (WPPSI, WISC, WAIS) for higher level TMR pupils.
3. Leiter International Performance Scale.
4. Goodenough Harris Drawing Test.
5. Peabody Picture Vocabulary Test.
6. Ammons Full Range Picture Vocabulary Test.
7. Raven Progressive Matrices.
8. Columbia Mental Ability Test.
9. Wide Range Achievement Test (when a measure of academic level is appropriate).

Subtrainable (Developmental Centers for Handicapped Minors - DCHM)

A recent trend is to establish programs for the subtrainable children, for whom no other school program is available. Still on a permissive basis, the humanitarian need for these programs is obvious. Though the children in these programs *need* not be retarded, the mere fact that they are ineligible for any other program usually means that retardation is present. As well as being of benefit to the child, these programs are of great help to the parents, as many of these youngsters are unable to care for even their basic feeding and/or toileting needs. Besides the humanitarian advantages, the *cost* of maintaining a child in these centers is far less than institutionalization.

Definition. Those severely handicapped minors between the ages of 3 and 21 who are ineligible for other special education classes, and who are declared eligible for DCHM placement by the Admissions Committee.

Eligibility. The determination of eligibility includes examinations given by a psychologist (or a psychometrist) and a physician. The minor may be eligible if all the following apply:

1. He is found to be ineligible for enrollment in a regular day class.
2. He is found to be ineligible for enrollment in special education programs.

3. He is found to have one or more of the following conditions:
   a. Serious impairment of locomotion.
   b. Severe orthopedic condition.
   c. Other severe disabling conditions which have as their origin mental retardation and/or physical impairment.
   d. Severe mental retardation.

4. The minor must be able to participate in at least one aspect of the program without danger to himself or others in the performance of daily activities.

5. Reasons for exclusion would include extreme hyperactivity, "dangerous" behavior, or a physical condition so sensitive that the individual could expire.

Placement. The child may be given a trial placement in a center after eligibility has been determined by an Admissions Committee consisting of a physician, a psychologist, a special education representative, and the DCHM supervising teacher. Factors considered by the Admissions Committee should include physical examinations and medical records, psychological tests, records of observations, family interviews, and previous school reports. If it is found, after a trial period, that the child is ineligible, the Admissions Committee also performs this function.

Class Size. Classes are usually limited to 10, with each class having a teacher (or permit teacher) and a teacher aide. The total program at each DCHM has a fully credentialed supervising teacher who is responsible for the supervision of the program. The supervising teacher should not teach a class when the center contains three or more classes.

Purpose and Goals

1. To provide training for children for whom no special education facilities are available. Most of these children are mentally retarded and many suffer physical handicaps as well.

2. To contribute to the mental health of the parents by providing respite from the continuous 24 hour care of their severely handicapped children.

3. To enable these children to develop to the maximum of their abilities.

Activities (Curriculum). The development center program provides for the supervision, instruction, and periodic assessment of each minor admitted to the center to determine readiness for transfer to other programs, continuance in the program, or discharge. Such services are usually offered for a minimum of 6 hours per day, up to 250 days per year. (Minimum days should be permitted for those not yet able to stay a full day). Program services include, but are not limited to, supervision, training, medical and psychological assessment, school nursing, feeding, speech, physical therapy, occupational therapy (when appropriate), transportation to and from the center, and parental counseling.

The daily activities are adapted to children with differing handicaps and various levels of maturity and capacity; thus, the activities are as flexible as space and facilities permit. The variety of experiences should include those such as quiet and active play, individual and group activities, music and rhythms, nutrition, and play with manipulative toys and equipment. Safety and self-help skills are stressed, as well as those of communication, coordination, sensory awareness, social awareness, good citizenship, responsibility, and health habits. The activities are generally built around the philosophy of routine, repetition, and relaxation, in which each child is encouraged to develop at his own individual pace.

The school day, which is determined by the local governing board, is usually from 9 A.M. until 3 P.M. The school year is usually based on the calendar year, except for the various state and national holidays. A short vacation (approximately 2 weeks) is also given, usually during the summer.

Appropriate Psychological Tests. (according to nature of child's difficulty).
1. Stanford-Binet, L-M.
2. Pre-School Attainment Record (PAR), with parent or teacher as informant.
3. Columbia Mental Maturity Scale — Revised Edition.
4. Gesell Developmental Scale.
5. Merrill-Palmer Pre-School Performance.
6. Nebraska Test of Learning Ability.
7. Minnesota Pre-School Test.
8. Leiter International Performance Scale.
9. Pintner-Patterson, etc.

Educationally Handicapped

Programs for Educationally Handicapped Minors: Currently the second largest category of special education classes is for the educationally handicapped, a group of children with neurological and/or emotional and educational involvement for whom virtually no school facilities were available as little as two decades ago. This is now considered the fastest growing category of special education classes.

Children eligible for EH classes are those with normal (or above) intelligence who have learning problems attributable to neurological impairment or behavioral disorders.

Definition. A minor whose learning problems are associated with neurological and/or emotional involvement, and who cannot profit from regular full-time class placement.

Eligibility. An educationally handicapped minor is eligible for a program if he has marked learning or behavior disorders, or both, associated with a neurological handicap or emotional disturbance. His disorder should not be attributable to mental retardation. The learning or behavior disorder should be manifest, in part, by specific learning disability. Such learning disabilities include, but are not limited to, perceptual handicaps, minimal cerebral dysfunction, dyslexia, dyscalculia, dysgraphia, school phobia, hyperkinesis, or impulsivity.

Screening. Potential special education pupils described above should be identified by individual assessment and evaluation of school records or written reports that include the studies described as follows:

1. *Educational Case Study.* A study of the pupil that includes:

   a. The school history and education progress of the pupil including the specific measurements of his levels of academic functioning.

   b. Specific steps taken to assist the pupil in the areas of his handicap and the results of such assistance.

   c. The reason the pupil is unable to function in a regular class.

2. *Psychological Case Study.* A psychological case study of the pupil by a credentialed or licensed psychologist that includes:

   a. Early development.

   b. Identification of the specific learning and/or behavior disorders and the relationship of these disorders to his school achievement. Specific handicapping conditions must be described in functional terms sufficient to indicate the specific characteristics of the pupil's problem and to suggest the nature of an educational approach.

   c. Recommendations regarding methods and services from which the pupil may be expected to profit in the program and the results anticipated.

   d. Evidence attesting to average or above average ability range.

3. *Medical Study.* A medical study by a licensed physician and surgeon of the physical, neurological, and emotional basis for the pupil's learning or behavior disorders. The evaluation shall include:

   a. A statement that in the professional judgment of the physician there is a reasonable indication of a neurological handicap or emotional disturbance.

   b. A functional description of the pupil's neurological handicap or emotional disturbance.

   c. A statement, in the case of a serious emotional disturbance that the pupil is capable of participation in the educationally handicapped minors' program and that the pupil's behavior would not be inimical to the welfare of the other pupils.

4. *Other Studies or Reports.* Studies or reports from personnel in any other areas that the Admissions Committee deems necessary because of the pupil's specific problems. These include, but are not limited to, speech and hearing, English as a second language, socio-economic disadvantage, social work, and welfare and attendance. Absence of such reports indicates that the committee considers that such reports would not be significant in evaluating the pupil's handicap or in planning his educational program.

Admissions Committee. (See section on EMR). A physician is not required in most states.

Placement. Standards for the Admissions Committee recommendations are as follows:

1. The Admissions Committee evaluates each individual pupil referred to it by making a thorough study of the records and reports together with all other pertinent and reliable information available. A written report of the study is filed with the district. The report includes the following:

   a. The committee's findings regarding the nature and extent of the pupil's specific handicaps and the relationship of these handicaps to his educational and learning needs and ability to function in a regular class.

   b. The committee's findings regarding the particular educational approaches, methods, or services appropriate for the amelioration of the pupil's learning or behavior disorders.

c. The committee's findings regarding the ability of the pupil to profit from participation in the program, the anticipated results, and specific recommendations regarding the placement of the pupil in the most appropriate of such programs.

d. The committee's majority decision, with the school psychologist and physician concurring, that the pupil is recommended for placement. The statement of eligibility is included with the signature and role of each person present at the meeting at which the recommendation was made. Any dissenting member should attach a statement of reasons for his objection to the report.

2. The committee may withhold a recommendation for placement of a pupil in a program whenever the committee determines that it does not have sufficient information to ascertain the pupil's eligibility or to recommend placement.

3. The responsibility for assignment of a pupil to a program rests with the administrative head of the school district or the county superintendent of schools or his designee.

4. Assignments are made in accordance with the program recommended by the Admissions Committee. No pupil should be placed in a program, transferred, or discharged prior to the recommendation of the committee.

Parent Approval. Usually required. (Required in Calif.)

Annual Review, Reevaluation, Readmission, and Transfer. An annual examination and evaluation should be made of the school adjustment and educational progress of each pupil enrolled in a program. The administrative head of the school district or the county superintendent of schools (or his designee) specifies the personnel and methods to be used in the examination and maintains a written statement of such procedures. The procedures provide for consistency in the specific measurements used in determining academic progress. A written report is made of the examination and evaluation of each pupil, and a copy added to the pupil's case study file.

The report includes the following:

1. A summary of the development and progress since the last written evaluation report.

2. The results of specific measurements of the pupil's progress in the academic areas of instruction.

3. A summary of the methods and techniques which have been utilized in the instructional program.

4. A current revision of the description of the nature and extent of the pupil's handicaps and ability to function in a regular class.

5. Specific recommendations for the pupil's continuing education.

The Admissions Committee reviews the annual evaluation report of each pupil either on the anniversary of the pupil's admission or at the end of each school year. If, at the end of the admission period, the pupil is found to be unable to return to regular class, the committee again files the report.

A pupil failing at any time to make an appropriate school adjustment or satisfactory educational progress in accordance with the prognosis and recommendations of the Admissions Committee is referred by the chief administrator of the district to the Admissions Committee for recommendations regarding transfer or discharge.

Class Size. The maximum enrollment for special day classes for educationally handicapped minors is usually 12.

Curriculum Content. The curriculum of any such program should be established under the following provisions:

1. The curriculum is designed to fit the individual developmental level and learning needs of each pupil as determined and reported by the Admissions Committee. Adjustments are made to the curriculum as the pupil's progress requires.

2. The amelioration of the learning or behavior problems determined for each pupil is emphasized by giving specialized instruction in the areas of disability.

3. Adaptations in methodology are made in the presentation of instruction in the sensory modalities employed and in the performance required of each pupil, whenever such adaptations will enhance his learning potential.

4. The curriculum otherwise emphasizes fundamental school subjects. A course of study for educationally handicapped minors in high schools should be adaptable to the individual needs for each pupil and provide the basis for graduation requirements.

School Day. Special day classes are maintained for at least the minimum school day. The class is taught by a full-time teacher whose responsibility it is to teach pupils enrolled for the school day as established by the governing board for pupils who are in the highest grade level in the special class.

Learning Disability Group (LDG)

Definition. Besides the special day classes for educationally handicapped minors, those pupils who are able to spend a part of the day in regular classes may belong to a special learning disability group, receiving special instruction from a learning disability tutor. These pupils are screened and placed by the administrative head of the school district upon the recommendations of the Admissions Committee in a manner similar to the placement of educationally handicapped minors into special class.

Standards. A learning disability group should meet the following description:

1. It is composed of pupils whose range of handicaps can be appropriately managed within the group.

2. It is limited to educationally handicapped minors who are enrolled in one or more groups for instructional periods of at least 30 minutes in accordance with the recommendations of the Admissions Committee.

3. It provides specialized instruction for pupils in each group on a daily basis or, if less than daily, on a basis to correct the handicap in the shortest period of time.

4. It limits a part-time teacher of learning disability groups to a total that is in the same proportion to 32 as the number of minutes taught in learning disability groups is to the length of the regular school day.

5. It allows opportunity for daily preparation for the teacher to provide an effective program of instruction and coordination with the pupil's regular program of instruction.

Class Size. The maximum enrollment for a learning disability group should be eight pupils, except that in a group session in which the chronological age span is greater than 3 years, the maximum becomes six. The total enrollment assigned to any one full-time teacher should be no more than 32 pupils in kindergarten, elementary, or junior high school. He shall have no more than 40 such minors in high school.

Special Home or Hospital Instruction. Unless health or other factors indicate otherwise, a pupil enrolled in home or hospital instruction is enrolled for, and should receive, at least 300 minutes of individual instruction per week. In no event should a pupil be enrolled for, or receive, less than 150 minutes of individual instruction per week.

Special Consultation to Educationally Handicapped Minors. Such consultation should meet the following standards:

1. The consultation is given by specialists from such fields as education, speech, social work, psychiatry, medicine, and psychology.

2. The consultation relates to the specialized instruction, management, and guidance of pupils in a program, and to the in-service training of teachers and staff.

3. State allowances for specialized consultation are used only to provide specialists not regularly employed by the district or county superintendent of schools administering the program.

4. Expenses of identification and of the Admissions Committee are not paid from state allowances for specialized consultation.

Admissions, Placement, Review, Etc. (See section on Educationally Handicapped.)

Mentally Superior

Gifted minor programs

Definition. Those minors who have demonstrated such general intellectual ability as to place them in the top 2% of all students achieving at similar grade level throughout the state.

Eligibility. The pupil evidences general intellectual ability, in keeping with the above, by one or more of the following factors:

1. Achievement in school work.

2. Scores on tests measuring general intellectual ability and aptitude.

3. Judgment of teachers, school administrators, and supervisors familiar with the minor's demonstrated ability.

Placement. It is the responsibility of the chief administrator or designated employee with the recommendation of a committee, consisting of the school psychologist, school principal, a classroom teacher familiar with the child's work or another pupil personnel worker qualified to administer and to interpret tests of mental ability to consider placement based on:

1. A score of 130 or above on an individual intelligence test such as the Revised Stanford-Binet, Form L-M.

2. A score at or above the 98th percentile on a group mental ability test, and a standardized achievement test in *both* reading and arithmetic.

3. Parental (or guardian) consent.

Types of Programs. Most programs are one or a combination of two or more of the following types:

1. The child remains in regular class and participates in additional educational activities through advanced materials and/or receives special outside help.
2. The child receives correspondence courses or has special tutoring.
3. The child is placed in grades or classes more advanced than his chronological age with special outside instruction.
4. A high school student attends college or junior college classes part of the day.
5. The child receives planned special counseling or instructional activities carried on during or outside of the regular school day.
6. The child is placed in special enrichment classes in one or more subjects for part or all of a regular school day.

Physically Handicapped

Deaf and Severely Hard of Hearing

Pupils assigned to classes for the deaf and severely hard of hearing are those whose auditory loss is so profound as to seriously impair their ability to interpret oral communication without special help.

Definition. A minor should be considered deaf if he comes within any of the following descriptions:

1. He has a hearing loss in the better ear that is from 70 decibels in the speech range to inability to distinguish more than two frequencies at the highest measurable level of intensity, with the result that he cannot understand and acquire speech and language through the sense of hearing, even with sound amplification.
2. He has a hearing loss in his better ear that averages 50 or more decibels in the speech range and, because he sustained the loss from babyhood or very early childhood, does not learn language and speech through the unaided ear.
3. In the combined opinion of a hearing specialist and a qualified educator, he would benefit from the special educational facilities provided for deaf minors.

A minor should be considered severely hard of hearing if he comes within any of the following descriptions:

1. He has a hearing loss in his better ear that is from 45 to 70 decibels in the speech range and, as a result, suffers delayed speech and language development to such an extent as to hamper his progress in a regular classroom at a rate commensurate with his intellectual ability.
2. He has a hearing loss in his better ear that averages more than 30 decibels in the speech range, the loss has been diagnosed by a licensed physician and surgeon to be progressive in nature, and the minor, because of delayed speech and language development, has the need for placement in a special day class or integrated program.
3. He has a hearing loss in his better ear that averages more than 30 decibels in the speech range, the loss was sustained in babyhood or early childhood, and it has resulted in delayed speech and language development.

A minor is considered moderately hard of hearing when *all* the following apply to him:

1. He has a hearing loss in the better ear from 20 to 40 decibels in the speech range.
2. His speech or language is impaired and such impairment presumably is associated with his hearing loss.
3. His hearing loss interferes with his progress in a regular classroom.
4. His individual and educational needs indicate placement in a remedial class.
5. A licensed physician and surgeon, audiologist, or teacher (or specialist) holding a certificate in the area of the speech and hearing handicapped has assessed the extent of the minor's hearing impairment and has recommended that he receive remedial instruction.

Eligibility for Programs and Services. The governing board of a school district establishes regulations determining who can profit by and who shall receive the special instruction. Specific policies and procedures should be established and maintained by the governing board of a school district or by the county superintendent of schools.

School Programs Available for the Deaf and Hard of Hearing.

1. **Special Day Class.** A special day class should have *all* of the following characteristics:
   a. The class is established for a group of pupils with similar handicapping conditions, listed above under "Definition." Deaf and severely hard of hearing may be combined.
   b. Each pupil enrolled attends school for at least the minimum school day necessary for determining a day of attendance for him.

c. Each pupil enrolled in the class is scheduled in the special day class for at least three-fourths of the minimum school day for that pupil's grade level.

d. The class is taught by a full time teacher whose responsibility is to teach pupils enrolled in the class for the school day established by the governing board for regular classes for the grade level of that pupil in the special class who is at the highest grade level.

2. **Other Instructional Methods or Organization.**

a. *Regular Day Class Without Integrated Program.* A deaf or hard of hearing (or blind or partially seeing) pupil enrolled in a regular day class for which expenses are incurred for special services such as supplemental teaching, transportation, teaching aids, and equipment over and beyond services provided pupils not determined to be physically handicapped may, in order to benefit fully from the regular class instruction, be taught in the regular day class.

b. *Regular Day Class With Integrated Program.* An integrated program of instruction in which physically handicapped minors receive their education in a regular classroom from regular teachers, but receive, in addition, supplementary teaching services from a full time special teacher. The supplementary teaching services may include instruction in the appropriate tool skills, the provision of special materials and use of special equipment, the guidance necessary to enable physically handicapped children and those handicapped in vision and hearing to benefit fully from their instruction. Pupils in integrated programs are counted and reported under "regular day classes."

c. *Remedial Classes.* A remedial class is a class providing to physically handicapped minors who are excused in small numbers for not to exceed a class period of 1 hour from regular classes or summer school classes, one of the following:

(1) Remedial instruction in other than physical education.

(2) Instruction in *remedial* (formerly "special") physical education to pupils.

d. *Individual Instruction.* Individual instruction is that which a teacher gives to an individual physically handicapped minor in:

(1) Hospitals, sanatoriums, preventoriums, in the home, at the bedside in institutions.

(2) The school, in the case of a minor with speech deviations at the age of 3 years.

(3) The school or the home, in the case of a deaf or severely hard of hearing minor between 3 and 6 years of age if there are fewer than five such educable minors in the community, making the establishment of special day classes impractical.

(4) An experimental program conducted for deaf or severely hard of hearing youngsters between 18 months and 3 years of age (now available in most states).

e. *Other Means.* Any other means of instructing a physically handicapped minor that is approved by the State Department of Education.

Class Size. (Special Day Class). The number of pupils enrolled in a class at any given time constitutes the size of the class. The appropriate size of a special day class is as follows:

1. *Deaf.* Age pre-school through 8 years, *6.* Ages 9 through 20, 8.

2. *Severely Hard of Hearing.* Age pre-school through 8 years, 8. Ages 9 through 20, *10.*

3. *Deaf and Severely Hard of Hearing combined.* Age pre-school through 8 years, *6.* Ages 9 through 20, *8.*

4. A class in which there are pupils below *and* above 9 years of age enrolled should be that size specified for the age pre-school through 8 years, a maximum of *6.* Any increase of enrollment above the appropriate size should be made only on prior written approval of the State Superintendent of Public Instruction in request initiated after the opening of the school year.

School Day. The recommended length of the minimum school day is: 200 minutes for kindergarten, 230 minutes for primary grades 1 through 3, 240 minutes for grades 4 through 12, 60 minutes for individual instruction. The 5 minute break required for each hour should not be counted in these minimum day lengths, nor should recess or the lunch period. The prescribed minimum days include instruction only.

Age Limits.

1. Mandatory Programs: All pupils age 6 to 21 years.

2. Permissive Programs: All pupils 3 to 6 years. Experimental programs for ages 18 months to 3 years.

3. All ages are computed as of September 1.

Curriculum. Except for a few specialized areas such as music, the curriculum for the deaf does not differ from that of the regular class. The differences are in the method of instruction, the rate of progress in the subject matter areas, the relationship of the material to language development, and the emphasis on communication skills. Besides the regular curriculum, there is intensive and technical instruction in the following basic skill areas.*

1. *Auditory Training.* Discrimination among gross sounds, between vowels and consonants, etc.

2. *Speechreading.* Sometimes referred to as lipreading, the pupil learns lip, teeth, and tongue position in the formation of sounds being uttered.

3. *Speech.* The age at which a child lost his hearing usually determines the nature and type of training.

4. *Language.* Using all the sensory channels possible.

Appropriate Psychological Tests. **

1. *Performance Tests.*
   a. Arthur Point Scales (ages about 6 and older).
   b. Cornell-Coxe Performance Ability Scale (ages 4½ through 16).
   c. Drever-Collins Performance Scale.
   d. Leiter International Performance Scale (three tests, ranging from ages 2 through 18).
   e. Nebraska Test of Learning Ability (ages 4 through 10).
   f. Pintner-Patterson Performance Scale (ages 4 through 16).
   g. Ontario School Ability Examination (ages 5 through 17).
   h. Wechsler Intelligence Scale for Children, performance section (ages 5 through 15).
   i. Wechsler Adult Intelligence Scale, performance section (ages 16 and above).

2. *Non-Language Tests*
   a. Pintner General Ability Tests: Non-Language Series (ages pre-school through college).
   b. Chicago Non-Verbal Examination (ages about 8 through 14).
   c. Goodenough Draw-A-Man Test (ages 3½ through about 12).

Placement in Regular Classes. Because deaf pupils at the elementary level usually do not have the necessary language development, speech growth, reading skills, etc., placement in a regular class on either a part-time or a full-time basis should be considered only when there is evidence that the child is able to profit from the instruction in the class. The following criteria have been suggested by the California State Department of Education, Bureau of Physically Exceptional Children:

1. The student is able to participate at or near the grade level of the regular class in using the receptive and expressive skills, such as speechreading, speech, language, reading, and writing.

2. The student's level of social and emotional maturity is at least equal to that of students in the regular class to which the assignment is to be made.

3. The student gives attention to the job at hand and follows directions well.

4. The student is sufficiently independent, self-confident, and determined to function successfully in the regular class program.

5. The student's ability to learn, as determined by the results of a standardized test, is average or above average.

6. The student's chronological age is within 2 years of the average age of the students in the regular class.

7. The students of the regular class will accept the deaf student as a member of the class, and will treat him with respect and consideration.

8. The teacher of the regular class understands the problems faced by the deaf student and is prepared to help the student solve his problems.

9. The enrollment of the regular class is sufficiently limited to permit the teacher to have opportunity to provide the special help needed by the deaf.

10. Appropriate sound amplification is available for the student's use in the regular class.

11. The family of the deaf student is interested in having him assigned to a regular class, will help him with his regular assignments as much as possible, and will help him solve problems he

---

*Adapted from "A Guide to the Education of the Deaf in the Public Schools of California," Cal. State Dept. of Education, 1967.

**Adapted from "A Guide to the Education of the Deaf in the Public School of California," Cal. State Dept. of Education, 1967.

may encounter in adjusting to the environment of the regular class.

12. The deaf student is willing and reasonably eager to accept assignment to the regular class.

Even in junior and senior high school, equivalent consideration of the various difficulties must be made for each pupil. Practically all deaf and hard of hearing pupils will continue to need the help of the special class teacher if they are to be successful in part-time assignments to regular class.

Aphasic

An aphasic child is one whose learning problems are due to receptive or expressive disorders in communication. The most clearcut characteristic is the inability to use language meaningfully. The diagnostic process is difficult, and children are often misplaced in classes for the retarded or emotionally disturbed.

Definition. A minor is considered aphasic when all the following conditions apply to him:

1. He has a severe speech and language disability.

2. The dysfunction or impairment is evidenced by a written diagnosis or determination (as appropriate) of aphasia or probable aphasia by each of the following:

   a. A licensed physician and surgeon who has training and experience in working with children who have neurological defects.

   b. A credentialed or certified psychologist.

   c. A teacher (or specialist) credentialed in the area of speech and hearing handicaps or a member of the staff of a speech and hearing clinic or center who is certificated by the American Speech and Hearing Association.

3. The disability is diagnosed or determined (as appropriate) by each of the persons described above to be other than a speech and language disability associated with deafness, mental retardation, or autism, and to be of an expressive, receptive, or integrative character or any combination of such characters.

4. The disability is of such severity as to require enrollment in a special day class, individual instruction, or special instruction.

Placement. The recommended steps for admission to these classes are:

1. Referral of the case by the administrator of the school district.

2. Each of the following persons must diagnose the case as aphasia or probably aphasia and must evidence this by a written statement (see 2a, 2b, and 2c above).

3. Parent's consent.

4. Review by the Admissions Committee (see Admissions Committee under EMR).

School Programs Available for the Aphasic

1. *Special Day Classes* (similar to same provisions for deaf and hard of hearing).

2. *Other Instructional Methods or Organization* (similar to same provisions for deaf and hard of hearing).

Class Size. (Special Day). The number of pupils enrolled in a class at any given time constitutes the size of the class. The appropriate sizes for special day classes for the aphasic are as follows: ages pre-school through 8, 6; ages 9 through 20, 8. A class in which there are pupils below *and* above 9 years of age shall be that size specified for the pre-school through age 8, a maximum of 6.

Any increase of enrollment above the appropriate size should be made only on prior written approval of the State Superintendent of Instruction in request initiated after the opening of the school year.

School Day, Age Limits: (Same as similar section on deaf and hard of hearing).

Blind and Partially Seeing

These classes are established for blind and partially sighted youngsters whose visual impairment is such that specialized materials and methods of instruction are needed. Special day classes are for those pupils who need a more intense and concentrated specialized program of instruction. Those who need only periodic help and special materials are served in the itinerant program. Mobility instruction is offered to blind and "legally blind" students to teach them to recognize cues that will permit them to move more safely in their home, school, and community.

Definition. A minor is considered blind who comes within either of the following descriptions:

1. His visual acuity in the better eye, after the best correction, is 20/200 or less.

2. His visual loss is so severe that, for educational purposes, vision cannot be used as a major channel of learning.

A minor is partially seeing who comes within either of the following descriptions:

1. His visual acuity is 20/70 or less in the better eye, after the best correction, and he can use vision as a major channel of learning.

2. His vision deviates from the normal to such an extent that, in the combined opinion of a qualified educator and either a physician and surgeon or an optometrist, he can benefit from special educational facilities provided for partially seeing children.

Classroom Clues Leading to Referral. Partially seeing children often go unnoticed unless their condition is severe enough to cause attention. The classroom teacher or psychologist should be aware of the following clues, which could serve as a basis for a referral: The partially seeing child frequently blinks his eyes more often, becomes confused or irritable doing close work, stumbles easily over small objects, rubs his eyes frequently, frowns more often, attempts to brush away blurs, is sensitive to light, has difficulty diffusing colors, often covers one eye when looking at books, or tends to tilt his head forward.

School Programs Available for the Blind and Partially Seeing.

1. *Special Day Classes.* A special day class should have all the following characteristics:

   a. The class is established for a group of pupils with similar handicapping conditions. Blind and partially seeing may be combined.

   b. Each pupil enrolled attends school for at least the minimum school day necessary for determining a day of attendance for him.

   c. Each pupil enrolled in the class is scheduled in the special day class for at least ¾ of the minimum school day for that pupil's grade level.

   d. The class is taught by a full time teacher whose responsibility it is to teach pupils enrolled in the class for the school day established by the governing board for regular classes at the grade level of that pupil in the special class who is at the highest grade level.

2. *Other Instructional Methods or Organizations.* (similar to same provisions for deaf and hard of hearing).

Class Size. (Special Day Class). The number of pupils enrolled in a class at any given time constitutes the size of the class. The appropriate sizes of special day classes for the blind and partially sighted should be approximately as follows:

1. *Blind*: ages pre-school through 8 years, 8; ages 9 through 20, 10.

2. *Partially Seeing*: ages pre-school through 8, 10; ages 9 through 20, 12.

3. *Blind and partially seeing combined*: ages pre-school through 8, 8; ages 9 through 20, 10.

A class in which there are pupils below *and* above age 9 years enrolled shall be the size specified for the pre-school through age 8, a maximum of 8.

An increase of enrollment above the appropriate size should be made only on prior written approval of the State Superintendent of Public Instruction in request initiated after the opening of the school year.

School Day. (Similar to same provisions for the deaf and hard of hearing.)

Appropriate Psychological Tests

1. Wechsler Intelligence Scale for Children, verbal section (ages 5 through 15).

2. Wechsler Adult Intelligence Scale, verbal subsection (ages 16 and above).

3. Stanford-Binet, L-M., verbal subtests (ages 2 through adult).

4. Hayes-Binet.

Age Limits

1. *Mandated Programs*: all pupils between 6 and 21 years.

2. *Permissive Programs*:
   a. All pupils between ages 3 and 6.
   b. Special experimental program between ages 18 months and 3 years.

3. All ages are determined as of September 1st.

Orthopedically Handicapped (OH)

Definition. Any minor who, by reason of a physical impairment, cannot receive the full benefit of ordinary education facilities, is considered a physically handicapped individual. This broad definition of "physically handicapped minors" includes the orthopedically handicapped. More specifically, the orthopedically handicapped children are those whose locomotion has been severely impaired due to crippling (and has been diagnosed by a competent physician) by one or more of the following: birth injuries, congenital anomalies, traumas, infections, developmental diseases, and other conditions such as fragile bones or muscular dystrophy. Physical and occupational therapy are available through the Department of Public Health, Division of Crippled Children's Services.

Eligibility. The physically handicapped child with one of the diagnoses listed above, who is not classified as mentally retarded, and who is between the ages of 3 and 21 may be considered eligible for OH placement. Other physically impaired children having mobility problems resulting from conditions such as uncontrolled epilepsy, severe cardiac impairment, and, sometimes, hemophilia, may be considered for placement in an OH class when it is impossible to make adequate provision for them in regular class. Admission of pre-school children (ages 3 to 5) to OH classes is necessarily on a trial basis, since the frequent complications of the multiple handicaps makes the educational planning difficult at this age.

Placement. There are certain special considerations for placement of a child in an OH class. The pre-school period, for example, should include a sufficient trial period to evaluate the child's physical, mental, and emotional development. Children of this age who are formally admitted should be capable of profiting from the pre-elementary curriculum being offered. First priority should be given to children needing physical, occupational, and speech therapy. Placement should depend also on the severity of the handicaps. Following are some considerations involved in the screening and placement:

1. Impairment of auditory, visual, kinesthetic, and tactual functioning, as a factor in the intellectual level of functioning.

2. The majority of these children are retarded in motor development to the extent that a delay of 12 to 14 months beyond the standard norms of motor development is not unusual.

3. The children must have some means of communication.

4. The children must be matured socially to the extent that their behavior does not endanger themselves or the others of the group.

5. Children who are severely mentally retarded as well as orthopedically handicapped are not eligible for placement in an OH class, and are usually more appropriately placed in a DCHM program.

6. The responsibility of assignment of children to the pre-elementary program for OH children rests with the administrative head of the district or his designee.

Class Size. The maximum enrollment should be 18, if the chronological age span is not greater than 4 years, and 15 if the age span is greater than 4 years.

Non-severely handicapped cerebral palsied children may be included in the class, as long as the number of children with cerebral palsy is less than half the total number of children in the room. (If more than one-half the number of children in the class have cerebral palsy, the class then becomes one for cerebral palsied children, and the total number allowed becomes 15, rather than 18).

OH Provisions at the Secondary Level.* Now that programs for the elementary level have become fairly well established nationally, districts are becoming concerned with the lack of facilities at the secondary level. The following are examples of alternatives some districts are adopting:

1. *Adaptations in the Regular Secondary School.* The OH student is allowed to attend a regular secondary school specially adapted for him. Adaptations include ramping doorways and curbs, scheduling classes so that extensive travel on campus is not needed, and providing monitor systems so that normal students can assist the handicapped.

2. *Special Classes Without Facilities for Therapy.* The classes are similar to those at the elementary level, but without the physical therapy. The student returns to the elementary facility to receive the therapy, on an out-patient basis. Transportation is provided by the district.

3. *Centralized Special Secondary Schools.* A large, specialized secondary school is developed, complete with facilities for therapy.

4. *Separate Homeroom.* A separate homeroom is provided, with the students participating in as many of the regular school activities as he is able.

5. *Secondary Program in the Elementary School.* In this case, the pupil becomes the financial responsibility of the high school at the age of the pupil's admittance to high school, usually at age 14.

Cerebral Palsied (CP)

Definition. The cerebral palsied, like the orthopedically handicapped, come under the broad definition of "physically handicapped minors." More specifically, and for purposes of their educational placement, the cerebral palsied are defined as "those children who have been diagnosed by a competent physician as having an impairment of motor function

---

*Adapted from "Educational Programs for Orthopedically Handicapped Children Including the Cerebral Palsied in California Schools," Cal. State Dept. of Ed., 1965.

by injury to certain portions of the brain which govern muscular control." Cerebral palsy characteristically causes such conditions as:

1. *Spasticity*: hypertension of muscles causing stiff and awkward movements.
2. *Athetosis*: constant, irregular, involuntary, and aimless motion.
3. *Ataxia*: lack of balance and poor spatial relations.
4. *Rigidity*: difficulty in extending arms and legs because muscles are partially contracted all the time.
5. *Tremor*: involuntary quivering or trembling of hands, arms, or neck.

Eligibility. Children, aged 3 to 21, with a medical diagnosis of cerebral palsy may be educated in classes for the cerebral palsied, or they may be included, if their condition is described as "non-severe," in classes for the orthopedically handicapped, provided that more than one-half the children in the OH class are not cerebral palsied.

Placement. Placement into a class for the cerebral palsied is similar to that for the OH children. There are, however, a few factors which make the educational considerations far more complex for the CP than for OH child. Children with impaired neurologic function, which is characteristic of CP, may have, in addition to mobility problems, a variety of intellectual, sensory, and behavioral symptoms singly or in combinations and in varying degrees. Further, the incidence of retardation is far greater in the CP than in the OH populations. The retarded child with cerebral palsy should be referred to the appropriate program for the retarded, or a DCHM program if the retardation is moderate or severe. In the case of a mentally retarded, cerebral palsied child, retardation is the *primary* diagnosis.

Class Size. The maximum class enrollment should be 15, if the chronological age span is not more than 4 years. If the age span is greater than 4 years, the maximum is 12. If the OH and CP programs are combined, the class should be designated as CP if more than half the pupils enrolled are cerebral palsied, or OH if more than half the pupils enrolled are orthopedically handicapped.

Itinerant Educational Specialists

Speech and Hearing Therapist. The speech and hearing specialist provides diagnostic and therapeutic service to individuals handicapped by impairments of language, speech, or hearing. In this sense, the work of this person is not the same as that of curriculum-oriented personnel.

Hearing therapy speech clinicians work with children on a weekly schedule determined by the nature of the child's problem. In most cases, the speech clinician travels to several different schools, and often even among several different districts.

1. *Identification.* At the beginning of the year, speech and hearing specialists generally conduct a survey in the school to determine which students need remedial assistance. This is usually done through an annual screening of selected primary grades. The general procedure in the upper grades is to operate on a teacher referral basis. Reports of the speech and hearing survey and diagnostic and assessment findings are forwarded to each teacher and principal.
2. *Placement.*
   a. It is the speech and hearing specialist's responsibility to determine which students are to receive remedial services. Preference is given those pupils who, in the professional judgment of the specialist, will not improve materially as a result of normal and maturational processes.
   b. Involves evaluation and initial assessment of the child's hearing.
   c. Involves notification of parents and arrangements for ongoing parent interaction.
3. *Scheduling.* Students are usually scheduled to remedial speech and hearing classes individually or in small groups according to grade, type of speech and hearing problems, and severity of the handicapping condition. Small groups of two or more students usually meet for a minimum of 20 to 30 minutes two or more times per week. Daily time schedules for students attending these groups or classes are established in cooperation with the building principal and teachers.
4. *Case Load.* The maximum number of individuals seen by each specialist each week is usually set at 90. This figure might be reduced proportionately depending on several factors: the number of schools involved, the distance between schools, and the number of times the children are seen each week. Children with more severe problems require more individual attention, which in turn decreases the number of children the specialist sees each week.
5. *Dismissal of Students.* A child should be dismissed from therapy when the specialist feels that the maximum benefit has been achieved. Dismissal depends on the accomplishment of the

therapeutic goals or objectives of therapy. Dismissal is considered a "tapering-off" procedure. Follow-up contacts are made with the child after dismissal to ensure that carryover is sustained and regression does not occur. Dismissal should be preceded by conferences with the teacher and parents. Children dismissed from therapy should be reevaluated periodically.

Home-School Consultant (School Social Worker)

There is a current trend toward the employment by a school district of a home-school consultant whose primary function is to work with the child through the home and community. Several districts, usually those with large enrollments, currently have such a person, who works with the school psychologist or director of guidance.

Qualifications. Generally, a school guidance credential, or an MSW, with a functional knowledge of the consultant role with demonstrated ability to put casework and group process training into practice.

Duties.

1. Assists district staff in developing a guidance approach for remediation for pupils whose behavior, including poor attendance, hinders their own learning and that of other pupils.

2. Diagnoses individual problems through a study of the pupil's learning process, responses to people in and out of school, his goals, needs and abilities.

3. Collaborates with other school personnel in a study of the pupil's particular school situation to determine changes in school handling which may improve learning and behavior.

4. Studies of the pupil's home and school environment to identify factors which may be affecting him and which may be changed to improve his learning and behavior.

5. Provides other case work and group work with the pupil and his parents as part of an educational plan.

6. Provides referral of pupil or his family to community agencies and services.

7. Maintains contact with community agencies and services, and assists in coordination and continuity of services in behalf of the child.

8. Consults with school staff on laws relating to children, court procedures, and relations with law enforcement.

9. Provides contact and conferences with parents.

10. Provides reports and maintains records needed for the home-school service, pupil personnel, and other district functions.

11. Participates in pupil personnel inservice training through district meetings and other professional groups and contacts.

Itinerant Teacher of the Gifted. (See section on the gifted).

Drug-Dependent

This new program in many states provides for special programs for drug-dependent minors. The California legislation on November 9, 1969, established the following criteria:

Eligibility. A drug dependent minor should be considered eligible for special education when all the following exist:

1. He is between 3 and 18 years of age, has not graduated from the 12th grade, and has not been attending regular or continuation school programs.

2. He is under the care of and has been identified by a licensed physician and surgeon as a drug-dependent minor who, because of such drug dependency, is unable to attend regular or continuation school programs.

3. There is on file in the district a statement by a licensed physician and surgeon and the county or district superintendent of schools or a person designated by him, that the minor is both safe for being instructed by a home instructor of physically handicapped pupils, and capable of benefiting from individual instruction.

Program and Place of Instruction. The minor may be enrolled in a program of individual instruction for the physically handicapped which may be provided at a suitable teaching station located in a hospital, clinic, or home.

Retention, Transfer, or Discharge. Retention, transfer, or discharge of a drug dependent minor from the program of special education shall be made by the county or district superintendent of schools or by a person designated by him, upon the recommendation of a licensed physician and surgeon. Retention in the programs beyond 1 school year may be made only upon the recommendation of a physician and the prior approval of the State Superintendent of Public Instruction.

Curriculum. The program of study shall conform as nearly as possible to that in which the minor was enrolled prior to his assignment to individual instruction. The program may be supplemented by counseling, guidance, and other specified instruction deemed beneficial to the student.

Credential. The teacher shall be a qualified home instructor of physically handicapped pupils.

Funding. Only those districts which have complied fully with the above can receive apportionment of funds.

Multi-Handicapped (MH)

A new program, in California at least, is that for the multi-handicapped, from ages 3 through 8. As of this writing, the guidelines for the program are still rather vague and the relationship of the MH to the DCHM program is not clear. The child, however, must have two or more handicaps, one of which may be mental retardation. It is possible that in the future the MH programs will lean toward the education of its pupils, while the DCHM will emphasize training and development.

A current trend is toward placing a school-age handicapped child in a private facility at school district expense when *no* appropriate public school program for the child is available. The private school must meet prescribed minimum educational standards, and may be selected by the school district, the parents, or the County Division of Special Education.

Secondary Pregnant Girls

These classes are for girls of high school age (14 years, 9 months or older), who are pregnant, and who have not yet finished their high school program. In addition to the regular high school program, courses in pre- and post-natal care are offered, as well as instruction in infant management. Although the program is usually not located on the regular high school campus or at the particular high school the girl formerly attended, there is an increasing trend toward having the pregnant girl (or even the young mother with her infant) attend regular classes with the other regular high school students.

Appendix A

Glossary of Terms for School Psychology

ACTING OUT: An expression of emotional conflict, (usually unconscious) or of strong feelings of hostility (or of love). The person is unaware of the relationship between the actions and his conflicts or feelings.

ACTIVITY GROUP THERAPY: (Slavson) A form of permissive play or group club activity in which children with behavioral or adjustment problems are given experience in group situations.

ADAPTIVE BEHAVIOR: An auto-corrective means by which we adjust to our environment.

ADJUSTMENT: An ongoing, dynamic, automatic process relating the individual to his inner self and his environment.

AFFECT: Emotional feeling tone. Often used interchangeably with emotion.

AGNOSIA: An organic brain disorder resulting in the inability to recognize and interpret sensory impressions.

AMAUROTIC FAMILY IDIOCY: A familial disease characterized by flaccid muscles, convulsions, muscular rigidity, and blindness. Also called Tay-Sachs disease.

AMBIVALENCE: The co-existence of two opposing drives or feelings toward the same person or goal.

AMENTIA: Mental retardation, usually organic, and due to a developmental lack of brain tissue.

ANABOLIC: Refers to the normal metabolic process of changing food to living tissue.

ANALGESIA: A condition in which the sense of pain is minimized or stopped.

ANECDOTAL RECORD: A short, factual and objective series of reports of a person's behavior, made by the observer. Often part of a case study.

ANOMALY: Abnormality.

ANOXIA: A condition caused by lack of oxygen in the blood, rendering tissue functioning inadequate. Cerebral anoxia, often a factor in mental retardation, is a lack of oxygen to the brain during the birth process.

APHASIA: A loss of ability to pronounce words or to name common objects. Motor aphasia victims may retain the understanding, but lose the memory traces necessary to produce a sound. It may also involve written expression. Sensory aphasia involves the loss of ability to comprehend the meaning of words or phrases. Cause is organic brain damage.

APRAXIA: A condition caused by lesions (cerebral cortex), resulting in an inability to perform certain physical movements.

ARMY GENERAL CLASSIFICATION TEST: (AGCT) (For grades 9-16 and adults). An omnibus group intelligence test with both handscoring and machine-scoring editions. Though considered useful in the military, most reviewers (Buros) are concerned with the lack of adequate norms for a civilian population.

ARTHUR POINT SCALE PERFORMANCE TEST: A performance test for children age 6 and over, often used with the deaf.

ARTICULATION: The movement of the muscles used in forming speech sounds.

ASPIRATION LEVEL: The life goal one sets for himself. The role of the counselor is to help the student set a realistic level for himself.

ASYMPTOMATIC: Showing no symptoms.

ATAXIA: Not having normal muscular coordination. A form of cerebral palsy.

ATHETOSIS: A condition in which organic brain injury (cerebral palsy) causes continual, slow changes of position of the fingers and toes.

AUDITORY DISCRIMINATION TEST: (Wepman) (Ages 5-8) An individual test designed to measure auditory discrimination ability in the young children. A quick, easily scored test, it is considered useful in primary grades for screening purposes.

AUTISM: Usually associated with children, and considered related to schizophrenia, this condition manifests itself in extreme withdrawal, stimulus reaction failure, lack of eye contact, and inappropriate verbal behavior. Prognosis is usually considered poor.

AUTONOMIC NERVOUS SYSTEM: The part of the nervous system not ordinarily subject to voluntary control.

AYRES MEASURING SCALE FOR HANDWRITING: (For grades 5-8) A standardized instrument for measuring a pupil's handwriting quality and speed, by being compared with samples for the various grade levels.

BENDER GESTALT TEST: A test in which the pupil is asked to copy nine simple designs from printed cards. Drawings may suggest perceptual distortion, psychological, or neurological disorder. Test is respected, but interpretation is limited to experienced examiners.

BLOCKING: Interruption in thought, memory, or speech, usually due to unconscious emotional factors.

BONE AGE: A means of predicting and measuring growth in terms of bone development, usually through wrist x-ray.

CALIFORNIA ACHIEVEMENT TEST: (Several editions, grades 1-14) A comprehensive group battery which gives grade-level equivalents in vocabulary, reading comprehension, arithmetic, English mechanics, spelling, and handwriting.

CALIFORNIA TEST OF MENTAL MATURITY: (CTMM) Short form: (Various editions for grades kdgn. through adult) A widely used group intelligence test used primarily with school children. The test is considered most useful at the lower grade levels, and progressively less useful at the upper grade levels (Buros).

CALIFORNIA TEST OF PERSONALITY: (Ages kdgn. through adult) A self-reporting inventory yielding scores in 16 areas of personal adjustment, plus a total social adjustment score.

CATHARSIS: A therapeutic release of ideas through talking or understanding of conscious material, accompanied by the appropriate emotional reaction.

CATTELL INFANT INTELLIGENCE SCALE: (Age 3-30 months) An intelligence test for infants; a downward extension of the Stanford-Binet.

CEILING: The upper limit of a person's ability on a given test.

CEREBELLUM: The part of the brain involved in muscle coordination and equilibrium.

CEREBRUM: The largest part of the brain, located in the upper region of the cranium.

CHILDREN'S APPERCEPTION TEST: (CAT) Ages 3-10) A personality test consisting of 10 cards depicting "family" scenes of animals, which the child describes. Administration takes only 10-15 minutes.

CHOREA: A nervous disorder manifested by involuntary motions (mostly facial), popularly called St. Vitus Dance.

CLIENT CENTERED: An approach in which the individual rather than the issue is the focal point. Client-centered counseling, as advocated by Rogers and others, requires a permissive atmosphere in which the client gains sufficient insight to be able to recognize and to take positive steps himself.

CLIMATE: Psychological atmosphere or feeling tone present in a classroom or group, determined by the individual attitudes within the group.

COGNITIVE: Referring to mental processes such as comprehension, judgment, reasoning, etc.

COLLEGE PLACEMENT TEST: A group intelligence test (both verbal and quantitative) for high school seniors and college students.

COLUMBIA MENTAL MATURITY SCALE: (Ages 3-12) A nonverbal test of ability utilizing the child's ability to point to a figure or design on a card which does not belong with the others. Often used with the deaf, cerebral palsied, or bi-lingual children. Children generally enjoy this test, which takes only a few minutes to administer, and requires virtually no motor performance, though the results should be used with caution.

COMPENSATION: A defense mechanism in which an individual attempts to make up for real or imagined deficiencies through superior attainment in another area.

CONGENITAL: A condition present at birth, acquired during fetal development or birth, but not inherited.

CONFLICT: The conscious or unconscious clash between two opposing emotional forces, desires, etc.

CONVULSION: A violent involuntary series of muscular contractions. (See Epilepsy)

CORNELL-COXE PERFORMANCE ABILITY SCALE: A nonverbal performance test of intelligence for children 4½-16, used primarily with the deaf or bi-lingual.

CRETINISM: An abnormal condition, usually congenital, caused by lack of thyroid secretion, and characterized by stunted mental and physical development.

CULTURE-FAIR INTELLIGENCE TEST: (Various editions, for ages 4-8, retarded adults 8-13, average adults grades 10-16, and superior adults). A group intelligence test which attempts to measure general ability independent of school achievement and cultural advantage.

CYBERNETICS: The science of studying automation and its effects on people.

DAVIS-EELLS GAMES: (Two editions, for grades 1-2 and for 3-6). A culture-fair intelligence test for urban children.

DEAFNESS: A hearing loss in the better ear of 70 decibels or more. One is termed severely hard of hearing if his loss in the better ear is from 45-70 decibels, or if his loss is greater than 30 decibels and he has a diagnosis of impaired speech and language development due to the loss. He is termed hard of hearing if his loss in the better ear is from 20-40 decibels, and he requires special attention in the classroom because of the loss.

DECIBEL: A unit for measuring the volume of sound, used as the unit for describing the degree of a hearing loss.

DEMENTIA: Formerly used to designate psychosis; now refers to organic loss of intellectual activity.

DEPRESSION: Morbid dejection or melancholy, varying in intensity from neurosis to psychosis.

DEVELOPMENTAL CENTERS FOR HANDICAPPED MINORS: (DCHM) State-supported centers for severely handicapped youngsters age 3-21 for whom no other school placement is available.

DEVELOPMENTAL TASKS: Refers to those functions which follow a developmental sequence, the successful completion of one leading to another (e.g., sitting, crawling, walking, etc.).

DIFFERENTIAL APTITUDE TEST (DAT): A comprehensive group test for high school and adult levels.

DISINHIBITION: Random, uncontrolled behavior, often associated with emotional or neurological involvement.

DISSOCIATION: A defense process which operates automatically and unconsciously, in which significance and affect are separated from an idea or situation. Many hysterical reactions (amnesia, functional paralysis, etc.) are forms of dissociation.

DOWN'S SYNDROME: A clinical category of mental retardation symptomized by an abnormal chromosome division and characterized in part by slanting eyes, broad, short skull, and short, stubby fingers (formerly called mongolism).

DULL-NORMAL: The IQ range of roughly 80-90. Children in this range are normally able to profit from regular class instruction, but many times vocational counseling and training before or during high school is indicated.

DURRELL ANALYSIS OF READING DIFFICULTY: A series of diagnostic reading tests, measuring speed and comprehension of oral and silent reading, listening, and understanding.

DYSARTHRIA: Impaired speech due to organic disorders of the nervous system.

DYSGRAPHIA: A neurological disorder resulting in writing difficulties, such as mirror writing.

DYSLALIA: A defect in speech caused by damage to the speech organs rather than to the nervous system.

DYSLEXIA: An inability to deal with printed symbols.

ECHOLALIA: An automatic repetition of words or phrases, most frequently found in connection with certain schizophrenic disorders.

ECHOPRAXIA: Automatic repetition of the movement of others, made by psychotic patients.

EDUCABLE MENTALLY RETARDED (EMR): Those mildly retarded persons who because of mental retardation are incapable of being educated effectively through ordinary classroom instruction. IQ range is usually somewhere from 50-70.

E.E.G. (Electroencephalogram): A recording of minute electrical impulses from cell activity in the cerebral cortex. Useful in identifying areas of cortical damage.

EMPATHY: An awareness of the feelings or emotions of another person and of their significance; opposed to sympathy, which is nonobjective and more often emotional.

ENURESIS: Bed-wetting.

EPILEPSY: A condition characterized by periodic motor or sensory seizures, often accompanied by loss of consciousness. Forms include: (1) *epileptic equivalent*, in which the symptom appears, but is not a convulsive motor attack; (2) *Jacksonian epilepsy*, with recurring localized convulsive seizures or spasms, and without loss of consciousness; (3) *grand mal*, characterized by gross convulsive seizures and loss of consciousness; (4) *petit mal*, minor, nonconvulsive seizures, often limited to only momentary lapses of consciousness.

ETIOLOGY: A term referring to the cause of a disease or condition.

EXPULSION: Permanent dismissal (usually for punitive reasons) from school, requiring board action in most states.

EUPHORIA: An unrealistic feeling of well-being, not consistent with appropriate stimuli. Often of psychologic origin; also common among toxic states and organic brain disease.

FANTASY: An imaginary sequence of events, normal in children, but generally considered an avoidance technique among adults.

FLIGHT OF IDEAS: A fragmentary skipping verbally from one idea to another before the last idea has been concluded. Often associated with emotional disturbance, and common among those with organic brain disorders or manic-depressive psychosis.

FREE-FLOATING ANXIETY: Apprehension or fear of most situations. The person is usually unable to explain his perseverative condition.

FUGUE: A form of dissociation characterized by amnesia or by a literal physical flight from a threatening situation.

FULL-RANGE PICTURE VOCABULARY: (Ammons) An easily administered, quickly scored intelligence test based upon a person's (ages 2 through adult) receptive vocabulary and his ability to relate the descriptive word to one of four pictures on a card (a set of 16 cards for each form, A and B). Similar to the Peabody Picture Vocabulary Test and the Van Alstyne Picture Vocabulary Test. Useful with the handicapped.

"G" FACTOR: Spearman's descriptive label for "general" reasoning or intelligence. The term "G" has come to be used by psychologists for describing so-called native or central reasoning ability, as opposed to specific intellectual functions.

GESELL DEVELOPMENT SCHEDULES: (Ages 4 weeks through 6 years) A scale for assessing the developmental status (rather than intelligence, per se) of infants and children. Considered more reliable after 6 months than during the first few months of life.

GIFTED: (Mentally Superior) Intellectual ability which places a student in the top 2% of students in the state at similar grade level.

GLOBAL: Referring to the "whole," the gestalt or total response, as opposed to separate aspects or functions.

GOODENOUGH-HARRIS DRAWING TEST: (Ages 3-15) A more recent version of the Goodenough Draw-A-Person Test, which measures a child's intelligence in terms of his ability to draw a person. In spite of the relative simplicity of the test and the danger of reading too much into the results, psychologists generally like the test, because of the ease of administration and as a validation of other test results.

G.R.E. (Graduate Record Examination): A series of college achievement tests, placing the student on national norms of college graduates. Often used as screening test for college graduate work.

GUILFORD-ZIMMERMAN TEMPERAMENT SURVEY: (Grades 12 and over) A personality inventory yielding scores in 10 areas of personality (restraint, sociability, personal relations, etc.).

HALO EFFECT: A tendency on the part of the examiner or observer to rate an individual too high or too low on specific traits or abilities.

HAWTHORNE EFFECT: The tendency for a person or group to perform at a higher level while being studied or observed, presumably because they are aware of the attention they are receiving.

HAYES-BINET: A verbal intelligence test, usually used with the blind. Based on verbal items of the 1937 Stanford-Binet. Not currently widely used.

HEALY PICTORIAL COMPLETION TEST:: (Ages 5 and over) An intelligence test with incomplete pictures filled in by inserting the missing part.

HENMON-NELSON TESTS OF MENTAL ABILITY (Revised Edition): (Four editions, for ages 3-17) A group intelligence test, with appeal because of its relatively short length and its predictive ability for school success. Believed to be more useful for school planning than for vocational or personal counseling.

HETEROGENEOUS GROUPING: Informal grouping of pupils without reference to similar abilities or characteristics.

HOMEOSTASIS: Maintenance of automatic metabolic or psychologic processes, optimal for well-being and survival.

HOMOGENEOUS GROUPING: Formal grouping with direct reference to certain similar abilities or characteristics.

HOUSE-TREE-PERSON TEST (HTP): (Ages 5 and over) A projective test in which the person is told to draw each of the above, followed by an oral inquiry by the examiner.

IDIOGLOSSIA: A condition other than delayed speech in which the child's speech is not readily understood by an adult.

IDIOPATHIC: Any pathological condition of unknown origin.

IDIOT: A term formerly used to denote the lowest category of mental retardation (IQ below 25), now termed severely or profoundly retarded.

ILLINOIS TEST OF PSYCHOLINGUISTIC ABILITIES (ITPA): (Ages 2½-9) An increasingly used test of children's linguistic abilities. Frequently used as a diagnostic tool by school speech therapists as well as by psychologists.

IMBECILE: A term formerly used to denote a person in the IQ range of 25-50, now referred to as Moderately Retarded or TMR.

IMPULSION: A chronic compulsive urge to commit unlawful or disapproved acts.

INTEGRATION: The organization of new and old data, emotions, etc., into the personality.

INTROVERSION: Preoccupation with one's self, thus reducing interest in the environment (the opposite of extroversion).

IOWA TESTS OF BASIC SKILLS: (Grades 3-9) A rather lengthy (approx. 5 hrs.) battery of school achievement tests. Widely used in schools.

IPAT: Used to denote any of the many test publications by the Institute for Personality and Ability Testing.

IQ: Literally, intelligence quotient (Mental age divided by chronological age times 100).

KNOX CUBE TEST: (Ages 4½ and over) An older performance test in which the subject repeats tapping patterns (by memory) by the examiner, using different tapping sequences with four blocks.

KOHS BLOCK DESIGN: (Ages 5 and over) A performance test in which the subject reproduces block designs from a card, using colored blocks.

KUDER PREFERENCE RECORD: (Grades 9 through adult) Shows subject's occupational interests by forced-choice items.

KUHLMAN-ANDERSON INTELLIGENCE TEST: (7th Edition) (Several editions, grades kdgn. - 12). A series of group intelligence tests, widely used in the schools and acclaimed for their excellent norms.

LABILE: Vascillating emotions.

LEITER INTERNATIONAL PERFORMANCE SCALE: (Leiter) A nonverbal performance scale for the deaf, nonverbal, retarded, bilingual, or culturally disadvantaged children ages 2-18. Rather cumbersome and expensive, but a highly respected, useful test.

LOBOTOMY: The treatment of serious psychiatric disorders by brain surgery (psychosurgery) in which certain brain nerve fibers are cut to reduce tension and distress.

LOGORRHEA: Compulsive, excessive talking.

LORGE-THORNDIKE INTELLIGENCE TESTS: (Various editions, grades kdgn. - 12). A widely-used intelligence test, used primarily in the schools. Reviews of the test are most favorable (Buros).

MACHOVER TEST: (Ages 2 and over) A projective test in which the subject is asked to draw a person, followed by a drawing of a person of the sex other than the first drawing. He is then asked to make comments about the drawings.

MacQUARRIE TEST FOR MECHANICAL ABILITY: (Grades 7 and over) A paper and pencil test measuring the subject's mechanical and spatial ability. Often used for industry.

MACROCEPHALY: A pathological condition in which the head is especially large and long. Often results in mental retardation.

MARIANNE FROSTIG DEVELOPMENTAL TEST OF VISUAL PERCEPTION: (3rd Edition) (Ages 3-8) An individual test designed to measure perceptual functioning. A useful school screening test, in that it identifies young children who might need special perceptual training.

MERRILL-PALMER SCALE OF MENTAL TESTS: (Ages 24-63 months) An individual intelligence test, enjoyed by children because of the quantity of performance items and the "game-like" nature of the scale.

METROPOLITAN ACHIEVEMENT TESTS: (Several batteries, grades 1-12) Group tests of general school achievement.

METROPOLITAN READINESS TEST: (Grades kdgn. - 1) A predictive test of first grade reading and arithmetic, useful in helping first grade teachers group their pupils.

MICROCEPHALY: A pathological condition characterized by an exceptionally small head and usually with severe mental retardation.

MILLER ANALOGIES TEST (MATS): A series of 100 difficult verbal analogy items, used mainly for college graduate study screening.

MINNESOTA PRE-SCHOOL SCALE: (Ages 1½-6 years) Though somewhat dated, this carefully standardized individual intelligence scale is still widely used.

MONGOLISM: See Down's Syndrome.

MOONEY PROBLEM CHECK LIST: (Several editions, grades 7 through adult) A personality questionnaire, covering several appropriate areas.

MORON: A term formerly used to denote the IQ range of roughly 50-70, now termed mildly retarded or EMR.

MOTOR-PATTERNING: A sensori-motor approach designed to "program" the brain by means of prescribed physical exercises. (Doman-Delacato)

NEBRASKA TEST OF LEARNING APTITUDE: (Hiskey-Nebraska) A creditable test which can be used gesturally with the deaf as young as age 3.

NEOLOGISM: A word or combination of words coined by a neurotic or psychotic person to express a complex meaning related to the person's conflicts; not usually understood by others.

NEUROLOGIST: A physician specializing in organic diseases of the nervous system.

NEUROPSYCHIATRIST: A physician who specializes in nervous or psychiatric disorders related to organic disorders of the nervous system. Literally, a combination of the fields of neurology and psychiatry.

NEUROSIS: An emotional difficulty usually caused by unresolved and unconscious conflicts, usually resulting in partially impaired thinking and judgment. There are innumerable classifications of neurosis, depending on the particular symptom which predominates. No loss of contact with reality is involved, as in psychosis.

NULL HYPOTHESIS: (Ho) A tentative hypothesis which states that no significant difference exists. At the close of the research, the Ho is accepted or rejected.

OEDIPUS (Edipus) COMPLEX: A repressed desire of a child or person for sexual relations with the parent of the opposite sex (usually a boy for his mother).

OPERANT CONDITIONING: Reinforcement (reward) of desirable behavior to insure repetition of the behavior, ideally leading toward a habit pattern.

OPTHALMOLOGIST: A physician who specializes in eye diseases and their cure.

ORTHOPEDICALLY HANDICAPPED (OH): Any child who because of physical impairment cannot receive the full benefit of regular classroom activities, and is thus eligible for special class.

ORTHOPSYCHIATRY: Child psychiatry, with emphasis on prevention.

OTIS GROUP INTELLIGENCE SCALE: (Various editions, for grades kdgn. - 16 and adults) One of the oldest standardized group intelligence tests still used. Easily administered and scored, though considered in need of revision and updating.

PARANATAL: Occuring during the birth process.

PATHOGNOMONIC: A group of symptoms related to an entity (similar to syndrome).

PEABODY PICTURE VOCABULARY TEST (PPVT): An easily administered, untimed test of ability, useful for ages 2½-18. The administration and scoring usually takes only 10-15 minutes. Caution is recommended in interpreting the norms. Similar to the Ammons Full Range Picture Vocabulary Test and the Van Alstyne Picture Vocabulary Test, though perhaps the most widely-used of the three.

PERCENTILE (P): A score expressing one's ranking in terms of the percentage of the population falling below the subject (e.g., the 20th percentile would indicate that of 100 people, approximately 20 would fall below the person and 80 above him).

PERSEVERATION: Behavior causing one to continue pursuing a task after the need for it has passed. Often associated with neurological damage.

PERSUASION: A directive therapeutic counseling approach.

PHENYLKETONURIA: (PKU) An inborn error of metabolism producing an inability of the body to assimilate phenylalanine. Causes irreversible mental retardation unless detected (infant urine) and corrected in the first few weeks of life. Infant urine tests are now mandatory in most states.

PHOBIA: An unrealistic fear, usually accompanied by a compulsive act, such as running, avoidance, etc.

PLAY THERAPY: A therapeutic approach to children's disorders in which the observation and interpretation of the child's use of materials and his fantasy in his games and play form part of the basis of the therapy.

PINTNER GENERAL ABILITY TESTS: (Grades 4-9) Group general intelligence batteries, with separate language and non-language tests.

PORTEOUS MAZE TEST: (Ages 3 and over) A nonverbal individual intelligence test, based on the child's perceptual-motor ability. Especially useful with the deaf, bilingual, culturally disadvantaged, etc.

PRECONSCIOUS: Referring to the data or thoughts not in the immediate awareness, but which can be recalled by conscious effort.

PRELIMINARY SCHOLASTIC APTITUDE TEST (PSAT): Grades 11-12) A condensed version of the Scholastic Aptitude Test (SAT) designed to predict college success of high school students. Widely used and accepted, as is the SAT.

PRE-SCHOOL ATTAINMENT RECORD (PAR): A recent (1966) adaptation from the Vineland Scale by the same author (Doll), used primarily to measure physical, social, and intellectual skills in those children under 7 who are difficult to test. An informant (parent or teacher) is usually used, as with the Vineland Scale.

PROFOUNDLY RETARDED: IQ range below 20 or 25, not generally measured with reliability. These children generally cannot become proficient in personal care or safety measures, always requiring 24 hour care and adult supervision.

PROGNOSIS: Prediction based upon current evidence.

PROGRESSIVE MATRICES: (Ages 5 and over) An individual or group test of perceptual ability, perhaps most useful as a screening test to determine whether additional testing is needed. The test was designed as an attempt to measure intellectual functioning (see "G" factor) through selecting a missing part of a design. Useful with the handicapped, as only minimal movement and communication are needed.

PROJECTIVE TECHNIQUE: A device (test, inventory, interview, etc.) in which the subject is asked to describe, invent, relate, etc., and literally projects himself into the response.

PSEUDO-RETARDATION: Refers to a person who tests at the level of the retarded, but who does not present the picture of any of the clinical categories of retardation. Causes may include emotional, cultural, academic, etc.

PSYCHODRAMA: A technique of group psychotherapy (Moreno) in which individuals gain insight through dramatizing their emotional problems.

PSYCHOGENESIS: Causation of a symptom or illness by mental or psychologic rather than by organic factors.

PSYCHOSIS: A severe emotional disorder, resulting in loss of contact with reality.

PSYCHOTHERAPY: A generic term for any type of treatment which is based primarily upon verbal or nonverbal communication, rather than by physical or medical measures.

Q-SORT: A method of personality assessment in which the subject sorts cards (into separate piles) with words or phrases which describe personality types.

RAPPORT: In counseling, the client-counselor relationship.

REACTION FORMATION: A defense mechanism in which a person engages in the opposite thoughts, words, or actions he desires, avoiding the desired for fear of disapproval.

REGRESSION: The partial (or symbolic) readoption of more infantile means of gratification. The person unconsciously "returns" to a stage in his development in which he felt more secure.

RELIABILITY: In testing, refers to the consistency of a particular test. To be reliable, a test should measure repeatedly with roughly the same result. Types of reliability would include Equivalent Form (such as certain standardized tests with Forms A and B, such as the Gilmore, the old Binet, etc.), Test-Retest, Chance Halves (using alternate items), etc.

Rh INCOMPATIBILITY: A new blood group found to be identical with a blood factor found in the Rhesus monkey (hence the name Rh). When an incompatibility exists between the mother and the father (e.g., positive and negative) mental retardation can result. The discovery of the Rh factor has not only made the giving of blood transfusions a much safer process, but has also made possible the correction and treatment of the difficulty (hemolytic anemia of the newborn) caused by the Rh incompatibility.

REPRESSION: A mechanism in which the person rejects from the conscious level any unbearable thoughts or impulses. Though the thoughts are buried in the unconscious, they may emerge in disguised form.

RESISTANCE: An individual's psychological defense against bringing repressed thoughts, ideas, etc., into his awareness.

ROLE-PLAYING: A technique for developing insight through "acting-out" various situations similar to the person's own situation or problem.

RORSCHACH TEST: (Inkblot) A respected projective test using 10 symmetrical ink-blot designs as the clue. The subject describes what he sees on each card. The test requires an experienced examiner with special training in Rorschach.

ROSENZWEIG PICTURE-FRUSTRATION STUDY: A projective test in which the subject is shown cards depicting frustrating situations, and is asked what he thinks the person depicted might be saying.

RUBELLA: German measles, when suffered by the mother during the 1st trimester of pregnancy, frequently causing mental retardation in the fetus, and suggesting abortion.

RUBEOLA: Hard measles. Immunization is now required in school pupils in many states.

SCHOOL PHOBIA: A syndrome in which the pupil resists or refuses to go to school. Symptoms often include tears, nausea, tenseness, or defiance. Causes vary, but are believed to be most often related to separation anxiety.

SCOTOMA: A "blind spot" in one's psychological awareness.

SELECTIVE PERCEPTION: The tendency to see or hear what we *want* to see or hear, disregarding other conflicting stimuli.

SELF-ACTUALIZATION: The optimal state, in which we accept ourselves as functioning at our capacity, and with a minimal loss of physical or emotional functioning.

SELF-CONCEPT: Essentially, one's total opinion of himself, which is believed to vitally affect a level of functioning. This impression is also influenced by our perception of the feelings others have of us (Combs).

SEQUENTIAL TESTS OF EDUCATIONAL PROGRESS (STEP): (Several editions, grades 4-14) Group achievement tests involving the basic academic skills. Often used to screen or to predict future academic success.

SPASTICITY: Tightness of the muscles causing spasms and an inability to control motor operations.

SRA PRIMARY MENTAL ABILITIES, Revised: (Several editions, grades kdgn. - 12) A group test of intelligence or ability in the areas of verbal meaning, perceptual speed, numbers, spatial relationships, and reasoning.

STANFORD-BINET, L-M: (Ages 2 through superior adult) Perhaps the most widely-used and respected of intelligence tests. Though the global IQ score, based on the mental age concept, is quickly losing favor as an adequate description of intelligence, the standardization was so well done that the test will continue to be called a "favorite standardized interview technique" (Buros). The IQ score measures primarily one's reasoning, or general intelligence, especially at the high school and adult levels.

STANINE: A means of placement on a 9-point scale, with 5 as the median (and a standard deviation of 2).

STIGMATA: The characteristics or marks of a given condition.

STRABISMUS: Inability to direct the eyes to the same point as a result of imbalance in eye muscle control (crossed eyes).

STRONG VOCATIONAL INTEREST BLANK (SVIB): (Ages 17 and over) A self-rating inventory, used for pursuing appropriate vocational interests, and based on the interests of those already engaged in the vocations.

SUBLIMATION: A defense mechanism through which socially unacceptable drives and behaviors are diverted into socially acceptable channels.

SUBSTITUTION: (Displacement) A defense mechanism by which unattainable or unacceptable goals are unconsciously replaced by more attainable and acceptable goals.

SUBTRAINABLE: Severely handicapped youngsters (often, but not necessarily retarded) who are ineligible for any other school program because of their handicaps (See DCHM).

SUPPRESSION: A conscious effort to overcome unacceptable goals or thoughts. Not one of the defense mechanisms, because it is a *conscious effort*.

SZONDI TEST: (Ages 4 and over) A projective test in which the subject is presented pictures of psychotic patients, and asked to select those he likes and those he dislikes the most. Test is somewhat dated.

SUTURES: Refers to the spaces between the bones of the skull; in the retarded, generally refers to the spaces which did not close normally.

SYNCOPE: Fainting.

TACHISTOSCOPE: A device for presenting visual recognition items for extremely brief periods of time. Often used for developing speed in letter, form, or word recognition.

TAY-SACHS DISEASE: See Amaurotic Family Idiocy.

THEMATIC APPERCEPTION TEST (TAT): (Ages Jr. High School age and over) A projective test in which the subject is asked to tell a story suggested by a group of pictures.

TOXEMIA: A bacterial condition in which the blood contains toxic or poisonous substances.

TRAINABLE MENTALLY RETARDED (TMR): Refers to those moderately retarded persons who can be trained to care for their personal needs, gain a certain amount of social independence, and eventually work in a sheltered workshop situation. The IQ range is generally somewhere between 25-50.

TRANSFERENCE: An unconscious attachment to others of feelings once associated with parents or older siblings. Often used as a therapeutic tool in the counseling relationship.

TRAUMA: Any severe physical or emotional shock or injury.

TREMOR: An involuntary shaking or muscular movement of the body, most often involving the head or limbs.

TRIMESTER: Three months, usually referring to pregnancy (e.g., first trimester, second trimester, etc.).

UNDERACHIEVEMENT: Achieving markedly below one's evidenced potential as opposed to *low* achievement, in which one merely performs *at* his low level of competence.

UNDIFFERENTIATED: In mental retardation, refers to causes which are unknown.

VALIDITY: In testing, refers to the extent to which a given test measures what it purports to measure. May be curricular, predictive, construct, concurrent, etc.

VAN ALSTYNE PICTURE VOCABULARY TEST: (Ages 2-7) Similar to the Full Range Picture Vocabulary Test and the Peabody Picture Vocabulary Test, this newer edition of the "original" test of its type is easily administered and quickly scored. As with the other tests, it has merit when its purposes are remembered. Is especially useful with the handicapped.

VINELAND SCALE OF SOCIAL MATURITY: A test (scale) which measures the social development of a child, and is scored with the aid of a parent or others as informant. Score is reported as social age (SA) or social quotient (SQ). Has been largely replaced by the Pre-School Attainment Record (PAR) by Edgar Doll, author of both tests.

WECHSLER ADULT INTELLIGENCE SCALE (WAIS): (Ages 16 and over). The most widely-used individual intelligence scale other than the Stanford-Binet, and considered by many to be a more valid assessment of "total" intelligence because of the various subtests, in which the verbal and performance areas are equally weighted.

WECHSLER INTELLIGENCE SCALE FOR CHILDREN (WISC): (Ages 5-15) An extensively used individual intelligence test for children, especially useful in the schools because of the massive research relating the subtest profiles to curricular remediation. Frequently, the verbal section is administered to the blind or the physically impaired, and the performance to the deaf, bilingual, or culturally disadvantaged.

WECHSLER PRE-SCHOOL AND PRIMARY SCALE OF INTELLIGENCE (WPPSI): (Ages 3-7) A downward extension of the WISC, not yet widely used.

WETZEL GRID: A chart providing a norm for height and weight for school children, often used as an indicator for children's physical development in keeping with the norms for his age and build.

WIDE RANGE ACHIEVEMENT TEST (WRAT): (All ages) An individual achievement test for virtually any grade level, including nursery, which gives grade-level equivalent scores in spelling, arithmetic, and reading. Easy to administer and score, the short test has suprising validity and is frequently given school pupils in connection with an individual intelligence test to correlate ability with achievement.

Appendix B

Remediation Based on WISC Subtests

Verbal Section

INFORMATION: Indicates the alertness of an individual, interest in his world, some reflection of the circle from which he comes, background of information from home and school, cultural background and experiences, etc. Low score suggests a need for word games, student-made dictionaries, notebooks, reports, field trips, class discussion about films, slides, current events, news, sharing, etc. Motivation is vital.

COMPREHENSION: This subtest reflects practical knowledge, social judgment, ability to organize, etc. Bizarre answers suggest emotionality. Build the child's self-concept to aid his independent thinking. Increase verbal communication, giving assurance that he is listened to and that his ideas are worthwhile. Discuss or role-play simple situations, such as reporting fires, calling police, greeting guests, etc. Use unfinished story technique to encourage creative independence.

ARITHMETIC: Reflects elementary knowledge of arithmetic, power of concentration, listening, and reasoning. Build on successes, teaching elementary basics, one skill at a time, reinforcing and overlearning. Student's attitude toward arithmetic must become positive. Too often, remediation is given in large doses. Improvement must be gradual and positive.

SIMILARITIES: Measures the ability of a child to do logical and abstract thinking. A low score suggests that the child is not able to generalize and categorize from material learned. Encourage the child to develop lists of synonyms and antonyms, to watch for differences between essential and superficial material, to rhyme, to think in categories. This subtest usually correlates the highest with the total score.

VOCABULARY: Reflects the child's verbal abilities, experiences, knowledge, reading, and range of ideas. A pupil's vocabulary is often a good index of his schooling and his general functional intelligence. Is often influenced by cultural disadvantage, bilingualism, paucity of background, etc. As with information, attempt to enrich the pupil's life through verbal experiences, field trips, explanations, questions, conversations, etc. Encourage the child to ask questions, to describe what he is doing, to make a dictionary, etc.

DIGIT SPAN: Score represents ability for rote and immediate memory, attention span, concentration. Is considered sensitive to emotionality and fatigue, and not especially related to general mental ability. Child needs instruction in listening, paying attention, concentration, rhythm, memory.

(Higher performance than verbal subtotal scores may reflect bilingualism, a low or under-achiever, limited experiential background, mild or familial retardation. Higher verbal than performance sometimes reflects neurological or emotional disorders. Wechsler feels that a whole discrepancy (over 10 points) is indicative of pathology. This view is not shared by the writer).

Performance Section

PICTURE COMPLETION: Tests visual alertness and memory, attention to details, ability to see the gestalt, basic perceptual and conceptual abilities, order. Low scores suggest a need for teaching from a gestalt (whole to part) approach, more attention to details through work on items such as maps, art work, compasses, etc.

PICTURE ARRANGEMENT: Tests sequence of order, social planning, humor, ability to anticipate. Mental defectives usually unable to score high. Low scores suggest need for a gestalt teaching approach, sentence completion or story completion lessons, games or sentences involving cause-effect relationships, effective planning, scheduling, etc.

BLOCK DESIGN: Involves ability to perceive and analyze form and pattern into component parts, logical and abstract thinking. Higher correlation with verbal abilities and total score than other performance tests. Believed sensitive to hasty or impulsive behavior and to neurological disorders. Remediation includes motor-perceptual tasks such as art work with geometric forms, flannel board work, figure-background training (such as the Frostig materials).

OBJECT ASSEMBLY: Reflects thinking and work habits, attention, ability to persist, to see the gestalt, creativity. Low score suggests a need for a gestalt approach, concept formation, encouragement to complete a task, organization, and planning (work habits). Encourage flexibility in the pupil (ability to change direction). Use perceptual items such as jig-saw puzzles, paper mache art work, pasting, cutting, construction, etc.

CODING: Perhaps the most predictive subtest of school success. Indicates ability to persist and to attend. Remedial reading is often suggested by low score. Sensitive to discouragement and being timed. Remediation includes reading and writing skills, tracing, paper and pencil tasks, kinesthetic or sandpaper writing. Hobbies, such as learning the Morse code, 'secret' codes, etc.

MAZES: Reflects ability to see the gestalt, to anticipate, small muscle control. Sensitive to neurological or emotional disorders. Use visual-perceptual approaches, such as the Frostig materials, paper and pencil tasks, etc.

Appendix C

Remediation Based on ITPA Subtests

AUDITORY DECODING: Indicates the pupil's use of receptive language. Base the remediation on participation in conversations meaningful to the child. Emphasize his listening to questions or statements (spoken only once) which require yes or no responses. Give sequential directions, such as the Binet subtest (IV-6, 5). Read a paragraph or short story to the child, and have him recall the meaningful parts to you. As the child improves, expand the length and complexity of the story, directions, etc.

VISUAL DECODING: This subtest involves the pupil's ability to absorb (decode) visual stimuli. Remediation should utilize visual exercises such as gestural instructions, completion of forms, designs, puzzles, etc., the child's description of the meaning of pictures, identification of missing parts of designs or pictures (e.g., the WISC Picture Completion subtest), etc. The goal is toward the child's ability to make increasingly subtle discriminations.

AUDITORY-VOCAL ASSOCIATION: Involves the child's ability to listen and to respond appropriately. Remediation gradually progresses from concrete to more abstract associations. Make frequent use of the concept of categories ("How many things can you think of that fly?" "In what way are a .... and a .... alike?", etc.). Use problem situations, such as in the Binet or the WISC Comprehension subtests ("What should you do if .... ?"). You might also use sentence completion games, story completion, analogies, etc.

VISUAL-MOTOR ASSOCIATION: Involves the child's ability to categorize according to form, color, use, sequence, etc. Remediation should include exercises in sorting, describing, sequencing, etc. Tasks might be similar to the WISC Picture Arrangement subtest, or to those in the Leiter, in which the child arranges pictures in proper order to make a meaningful story, or selects the picture or form which does not belong with the others.

VOCAL ENCODING: Indicates the child's ability to define, narrate, describe, etc. Remediation involves the use of the child's expressive language and encouraging as much speech as possible in appropriate categories. Use tasks such as having the child answer questions, talking into a tape recorder, sharing, mock telephone conversations, verbalizing solutions to situational problems, verbal descriptions, narrations, choral speaking or singing, etc.

MOTOR ENCODING: Reflects the child's ability in body and perceptual motor tasks. Remediation involves the child's participation in perceptual-motor tasks such as drawing, tracing, acting or imitating movements depicted in scenes or by others, work such as is found in the Frostig materials, mazes, learning to tap out the Morse code, tasks related to the WISC Coding subtest, charades, etc.

AUDITORY-VOCAL AUTOMATIC: Involves the child's ability to verbally reproduce and incorporate material. Remediation includes tasks such as the child repeating the teacher's sentences, slightly modified to make them appropriate for the child (e.g., Tchr., "Today I will drive my car to see my brother"; Child, "This morning I will ride my bike to visit my friend"); finding and repeating words which have similar meaning; having the child say the word missing from a well-known song or saying; having the child repeat and complete the teacher's unfinished sentence, etc.

AUDITORY-VOCAL SEQUENCING: Indicates the child's ability in verbal sequencing (memory). Remediation involves the child's immediate verbal recall, and includes tasks such as repetition (verbatum) of the teacher's sentences, memorizing sequences of words — such as the days of the week or months reversed, etc. As the child improves, he can be taught to remember the events (in sequence) in a story, or the old game of each child adding one object to a list to be remembered.

VISUAL-MOTOR SEQUENCING: Involves visual memory. Remediation includes verbal or performance tasks presented visually, such as copying bead formations, series of blocks, designs (as in the Binet Designs subtest), pictures etc. The child might also tell a story which had been presented in a series of pictures, copy words or designs which have just been erased from the blackboard, etc.

Appendix D

Partial List of Commonly Used Psychological Tests

Army General Classification Test (AGCT), First Civilian Edition, 1960.

Ayres Space Test, ages 3 and over.

Bender Gestalt Test, 1964, ages 4 and over.

Cain-Levine Social Competency Scale, MR's ages 5-13.

Caldwell Preschool Inventory, ages 3-6.

California Achievement Tests (CAT). Several forms for various grade levels.

California Q-Sort.

California Short Form Test of Mental Maturity, various levels, kindergarten through adult.

California Test of Mental Maturity (CTMM), 1963, various forms, grade 4 through adult.

California Test of Personality (CTP), various forms, kindergarten through adult.

Cattell Infant Intelligence Scale, 1960, ages 3-30 months. Downward extension of the Binet.

Children's Apperception Test (CAT), 1961, ages 3-10.

Columbia Mental Maturity Scale, MA 3-10.

Culture-Fair Intelligence Test (Cattell), age 4 through adult.

Developmental Reading Tests, 1961, four levels, grades 1.5-6.

Differential Aptitude Test (DAT), 1963, grades 8-13 and adult.

Draw-A-Person, 1963, ages 5 and over.

Full-Range Picture Vocabulary (Ammons), 1948.

Gates Advanced Primary Reading Tests, 1958, grades 3.5-10.

Gates Primary Reading Test, 1958, grades 1-2.5.

Gates Reading Survey, 1960, grades 3.5-10.

Gesell Developmental Schedules, 1940 Series, 4 weeks through 6 years.

Gilmore Oral Reading Test (Forms A and B).

Goodenough-Harris Drawing Test, 1963, ages 3-15.

Gray Oral Reading Test, 1963, grades 1-12.

Henmon-Nelson Test of Mental Ability (Revised Edition), 1961, several forms, grades 3-17.

Illinois Test of Psycholinguistic Abilities (ITPA).

Iowa Tests of Basic Skills, grades 3-9.

Junior School Aptitude Test, Revised Edition, 1960, grades 7-9.

Kuder Preference Record, Personal, 1960, grades 9-16 and adults.

Kuhlman-Anderson Intelligence Test, Seventh Edition, various forms, grades kindergarten through 12.

Lee-Clark Reading Test, 1958 revision, grades 1-2.

Leiter International Performance Scale, ages 2-18.

Lincoln-Oseretsky Motor Development Scale, ages 6-14.

Lorge-Thorndike Intelligence Tests, 1962, several forms, grades kindergarten through 12.

Machover Draw-A-Person Test (sometimes called Machover Figure-Drawing Test), ages 2 and over.

Marianne Frostig Developmental Test of Visual Perception, 1964, ages 3-8.

Memory-For-Designs Test, 1960, ages 8.5 and over.

Merrill-Palmer Scale of Mental Tests, ages preschool through primary.

Metropolitan Achievement Tests, several forms, grades 1.5-12.

Miller Analogies Test (MATS), 1959, candidates for graduate school.

Minnesota Multiphasic Personality Inventory (MMPI), 1951, ages 16 and over.

Minnesota Pre-School Scale, 1940, ages 1.5-6.

Minnesota Rate of Manipulation Test, 1969.

Mooney Problem Check List, 1950, various forms, grade 7 through adult.

Otis Group Intelligence Scale, 1940, kindergarten through adult.

Peabody Picture Vocabulary Test (PPVT), 1959, ages 2.5-18.

Porteous Maze Test, 1959, ages 3 and over.

Preliminary Scholastic Aptitude Test, 1963, grades 11-12.

Pre-School Attainment Record (PAR), 1966, birth-7 years.

Progressive Matrices (Raven), 1963, ages 5 and over.

(The) Quick Test, 1962, ages 2 and over.

Rorschach Test.

Sequential Tests of Educational Progress (STEP), various forms, grades 4-14.

Slosson Intelligence Test (SIT), 1963, ages 1 month and over.

SRA Achievement Series, 1962, several forms, grades 1-12.

Stanford Achievement Test, several editions, grades 1.5-9.

Stanford-Binet Intelligence Scale, Third Revision, 1960, ages 2 and over.

Strong Vocational Interest Blank, separate forms for men and women, ages 17 and over.

Survey of Primary Reading Development (SPRD), 1957, grades 1-3.5.

Szondi Test.

Thematic Apperception Test (TAT), children and adults.

Van Alstyne Picture Vocabulary Test, 1961, MA 2-7.

Vineland Social Maturity Scale, 1953, birth to maturity.

Wechsler Adult Intelligence Scale (WAIS), 1949, ages 16 and over.

Wechsler Intelligence Scale for Children (WISC), 1949, ages 5-15.

Wechsler Pre-School and Primary Scale of Intelligence (WPPSI), ages 3-7.

Wepman Auditory Discrimination Test, ages 5-8.

Wide-Range Achievement Test (WRAT), 1965, nursery school through graduate school.

Appendix E

Directory of Psychological Test Publishers

American Guidance Services, Publisher's Building, Circle Pines, Minnesota 55014.

California Test Bureau, Del Monte Research Park, Monterey, California 93940.

Consulting Psychologists Press, Inc., 577 College Ave., Palo Alto, California 94306.

Cooperative Test Division, Educational Testing Service, Princeton, New Jersey 08540.

Harcourt, Brace, Jovanovich, Inc., 757 Third Ave., New York, New York 10017.

Houghton Mifflin Co., 2 Park St., Boston, Massachusetts 02107.

Lyons & Carnahan, 407 E. 25th St., Chicago, Illinois 60616.

National Association of Independent Schools, 4 Liberty Square, Boston, Massachusetts 02109.

Personnel Press, Inc., 191 Spring St., Lexington, Massachusetts 02173.

The Psychological Corporation, 304 E. 45th St., New York, New York 10017.

Psychological Test Specialists, Box 1441, Missoula, Montana 59801.

Science Research Associates, Inc., 259 E. Erie St., Chicago, Illinois 60611.

Slosson Educational Publications, 140 Pine St., Aurora, New York 14052.

Teachers College Press, 1234 Amsterdam Ave., New York, New York 10027.

Thomas (Charles) Publisher, 327 E. Lawrence Ave., Springfield, Illinois 62703.

University of Illinois Press, Urbana, Illinois 61803.

Western Psychological Services, 12031 Wilshire Blvd., Los Angeles, California 90025.

Subject Index

Close the Knowledge Gap!

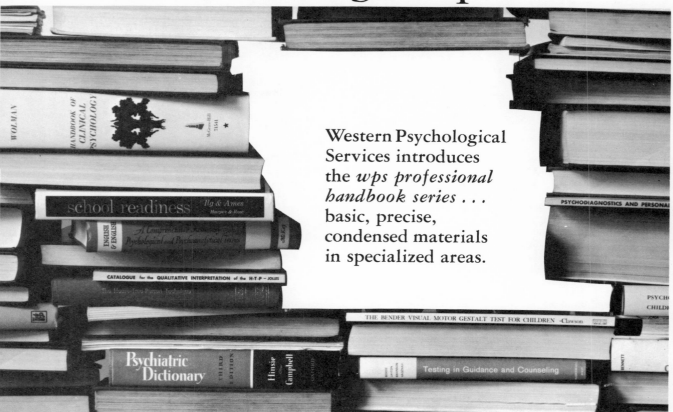

Western Psychological Services introduces the *wps professional handbook series* . . . basic, precise, condensed materials in specialized areas.

OVER

wps professional handbook series/3

INTELLECTUAL EVALUATION OF THE MENTALLY RETARDED CHILD: A HANDBOOK

by Robert M. Allen, Ph. D. and Sue P. Allen, M. Ed.
University of Miami   Special Education Department, Board of Public Instruction, Dade County, Florida

Widely used handbook on current concepts, techniques, procedures, and test descriptions for evaluating mentally retarded children. Discusses standard intelligence tests including: Wechsler Scales; preschool tests; picture vocabulary tests; formboards; drawing tests; non-verbal intelligence tests; paper-and-pencil tests; perceptual and psycholinguistic tests; tests for the blind; third person tests; and includes suggestions on the reporting of test findings. Has many illustrations, including photographs, of actual test materials and examples of widely used test forms. Paperbound, 70 pp (8½"x11"), **$7.50**

wps professional handbook series/4

A CLINICAL APPROACH TO TRAINING THE EDUCABLE MENTALLY RETARDED: A HANDBOOK

by Isaac Jolles and Selma I. Southwick
School Psychologist   Chairman, Program for Educable Mentally Handicapped
Fairfax County   Quincy Public Schools
  Public Schools   Quincy, Illinois
  Fairfax, Virginia

This handbook represents more than 20 years experience of a psychologist and a teacher who work with educable mentally retarded children. It covers the psychology, educational implications, and sensory deficiencies of these children. Presented are training programs for the improvement of perception, language and conceptional thinking, attention, and motivation. Also presented are classroom tested methods for teaching arithmetic, reading, and handwriting. Excellent handbook for all who work with educable mentally retarded children, especially their teachers, school psychologists, members of special education programs, and students. Paperbound, 31 pp (8½"x11"), **$6.50**

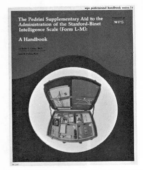

wps professional handbook series/5

THE PEDRINI SUPPLEMENTARY AID TO THE ADMINISTRATION OF THE STANFORD-BINET INTELLIGENCE SCALE (FORM L-M): A HANDBOOK

by Duilio T. Pedrini, Ph.D. and Laura N. Pedrini, Ph.D.
University of Nebraska
  at Omaha

A *detailed* handbook which supplements the test manual for the administration of the Stanford-Binet Intelligence Scale (Form L-M). Includes photographs of test materials for easy reference. Excellent as a training manual for the beginning examiner. Also valuable as a resource book for the experienced examiner. Paperbound, 50 pp (8½"x11"), **$7.50**

wps professional handbook series/6

THE SCHOOL PSYCHOLOGIST'S HANDBOOK

by Arthur A. Attwell, Ed.D.
Chairman, Department of Educational Psychology
California State University, Los Angeles

A *practical* and *useful* reference for the school psychologist presented from a school orientation in order to assist him in making meaningful and practical recommendations. It is an especially valuable handbook for the new school psychologist with information on report writing; remediation of subject-matter learning difficulties as well as a variety of other common disabilities. It also contains suggestions for handling referrals and the school psychologist's role in special education. The inclusion of a glossary of terms for school psychology; remediation based upon WISC and ITPA subtests; a list of widely used psychological tests and a directory of test publishers make this book useful every day. Paperbound, 77 pp (8½"x11"), **$7.50**